EVERY BUSH IS BURNING

EVERY BUSH IS BURNING

a spirituality for our times

JOAN PULS, O.S.F.

Foreword by Dr. Susan Muto

TWENTY-THIRD PUBLICATIONS

Mystic, Connecticut

North American edition 1985
Twenty-Third Publications
P.O. Box 180
Mystic, CT 06355
(203) 536-2611

ISBN: 0-89622-280-2
Library of Congress Catalog Card Number
85-51476

Cover design by George Herrick

Foreword

I have found in my own life and through conversations with others that people need more and more to see the connection between ordinary reality and extraordinary grace, between everyday events and the divine mystery manifested in them. As this sensitivity to the sacred increases, we desire to give high priority to the person-to-person relationship that exists between the pilgrim soul and God. Only through the strength derived from this bond is it possible to give ourselves in turn to the service of others in the world.

Sister Joan Puls, O.S.F., the author of this compelling reflection on an incarnational approach to spirituality, recognizes the centrality of the transcendent desire of humans to discover and name the connections between body and spirit, person and world, the inner life of prayer and the outer life of ministry and relatedness.

The burning bush within us — the awe disposition that never dies — keeps reminding us that there is more to life than material gain, more than status, accomplishment, and worldly fame. The author rightly observes that in Western society a high premium is placed on the pleasure principle and on the philosophy of functioning. Vital impulses and functional ambitions often obscure transcendent aspirations and inspirations. Thus we live in the tension of secularization and spiritualization. This book helps us not only to reclaim the world as the house of God but also to heed the call to seek union iwth our maker, to praise the Trinity, to proclaim the Good News of the Spirit's presence in the midst of the smallest particle.

Reading this message of hope, we recognize that there is no excuse for us to live as half persons, hollowed out and unable to hear the subtle whispers of the voice within the burning bush inviting us to shake loose from our complacency and enter the world of contemplation. God calls out to us in moments of solitude and human encounter to look again at the false gods we worship and to see that they cannot fulfill us. We are children of the light, so why should we go about living in the darkness? Is it not time to awaken from our sleepy deceptions and to turn toward the one who says, "I am the Way, the Truth, the Life"? According to the author, the "Holy Spirit does not reward our searching with instant or spectacular results. Rather, the Spirit waits for a vulnerable moment, a sign of recognition, a cracked rim on our closed hearts, and slips in, to promote out of a tragedy a time of conversion, out of a casual event a miracle of grace." Such an approach to life as prayer and prayer as life opens our eyes to treasures beyond our wildest expectations.

God understands that we are vulnerable and fragile, yet he inisits that we are his children, never to be abandoned, always to be embraced and forgiven. Such is the pain and the glory of being human. We are not angels but neither are we animals. Our lives may not be lived totally in the light because there is in us the tendency to sin, but our hope is forever to relight the flame. Success is not what counts, only the trying. Moses did not live to see the Promised Land, but he continued the journey to the end. We are light dappled with shadow, but that is not the whole story; we are also a redeemed people, lifted from the slumber of an egocentric existence to the life of the Spirit. Indeed, we stand on holy ground, and that makes all the difference.

Each chapter of this book treats a key facet of human and Christian living. The approach is both unique and universal, for Sister Joan at once personalizes the text with examples and narratives pertinent to her life while drawing observations and appraisals relevant to all who seek seriously to become children of the light. Clearly she is influenced by her Franciscan charism. Her fondness for St. Francis as a free person, able to recognize "new patterns in the human web and free to rush foolishly into a life faithful to the gospel," is evident throughout the text. Francis emerges as a model for all who would "offer others their fullest and best selves rather than their obsessions, ego-centered ambitions, and self-delusions."

One chapter of the book flows gracefully into the other. Beginning with a consideration of the sacramental nature of life as a whole, Sister Joan moves in Chapter 2 toward a description of our formation journey as a search for God's meaning in our daily situation and in our moments of encounter inwardly with the Holy Spirit. Formation does not happen in a vacuum but in dialogue with society, in a faith community, and, of course, in silence. One must also expect, as she points out in Chapter 4, that the life of the spirit includes crisis, conflict, even chaos, but all of this can be a condition for hearing anew the call of Christ and following the path of discipleship.

Paradoxically, as the author reveals in Chapter 6, freedom resides in complete obedience to the truth for which we have been created. For the Christian, freedom consists in becoming obedient to the elements of Jesus' life, in making visible the fruits of the spirit: peace, joy, faith, mildness, and like virtues. One of her most insightful points surfaces in Chapter 7 where she shows that the secret of spirituality is the uncovering of the life of "exchange" — "the visible interconnectedness that makes all creation *one*." This is the flow of life, the universal dance of formation, the mysterious interweaving movement of the world, which Christians celebrate as the Body of Christ.

Reading this book has been for me a great source of consolation. I invite each reader to be open to its contents in such a way that your heart too will be touched and transformed.

Dr. Susan A. Muto
Institute of Formative Spirituality
Duquesne University
Pittsburgh, Pennsylvania

Table of contents

v FOREWORD
   Dr. Susan Muto

xi INTRODUCTION

1 1. LIFE

10 2. SEARCH

26 3. FORMATION

44 4. CONFLICT

60 5. OBEDIENCE

74 6. FREEDOM

88 7. EXCHANGE

Introduction

I have been watching a gull's flight. A graceful form against the blue sky. A broad circle over the lake. A sudden plunge downward. Then an easy arc and a gentle descent onto the sparkling water. "Freedom", I muse, "is complete obedience to the element for which we were designed."[1]

I feel an urgency at this stage in my life to name the human expressions and vivid manifestations of our life in the Spirit. I believe that nothing human is foreign to the Spirit, that the Spirit embraces all. Our mundane experiences contain all the stuff of holiness and of human growth in grace. Our world is rife with messages and signatures of the Spirit. Our encounters with one another are potential sites of the awakening and energizing that characterize the Spirit. But so much goes unnoticed. We fail so often to recognize the light that shines through the tiny chinks and the dusty panes of our daily lives. We are too busy to name the event that is blessed in its ordinariness, holy in its uniqueness, and grace-filled in its underlying challenge.

Our individual lives reflect the parables of the sower and the seed. We experience our own cycles of ploughing and seeding and anticipating a harvest. Conscious of that process in my own life, I have gathered the fruits year after year, discovered new ground in myself and my surroundings, and tried out new methods of planting. I have waited for the first sprouts in a new season, and I have dreamed about sharing the harvest. Perhaps the seeds were sown in a favourite childhood haunt, an apple tree in Louisburg, or on my solitary walks to and from school. They were nurtured surely by my attraction to poets and hermits and gentle saints, and by my repeated desire to be still and see that God is God. The plant was tested perhaps by my years of study, of preparation in philosophy, of teaching. Pruned by my years of tortured inner search and desert dwelling. Quickened by energetic and conscientious efforts for justice and peace. The fruits endured and resurrected during periods of research and reflection and retreat-giving.

Some of the results of my harvesting are contained in these pages. They tell the tale of my own sources, of the gifts that have sustained and inspired me, of the adventure that stretches me still into unknown and uncertain territory. My intention is to

---

[1] Joan Cox, Storrington, England.

describe a spirituality that is "ordinary" and "everyday". I
believe that the "extraordinary" shines through the smallest and
simplest of our experiences. I hope to share in this book, in
multiple ways and through a spectrum of images, that every
bush is burning.

The seven chapters are woven together by their incarnational
approach and by the linkage of personal spirituality and a
spirituality for our times. The first chapter, on life as whole and
sacramental, is the basis and the context for the others. Chapters
two and three are related, for it is in our search, as individuals
and as communities, that we are formed and that we recognize
the influences that surround us. Likewise it is in our confrontations with evil and with the powers of darkness (chapter 4), that
we learn obedience (chapter 5). As we enter into our liberty as
human beings and as children of God (chapter 6), we uncover
the mystery and the path of exchange (chapter 7).

These seven chapters are my testimony and my response to
Paul's question: "I want to learn only one thing from you: how
did you receive the Spirit? Have you had such remarkable
experiences all to no purpose? Is it because you observe the law
or because you have faith in what you heard (and saw and
touched) that God lavishes the Spirit on you and works wonders
in your midst?" (Gal. 3:1-5).[2]

I share this journey with those of you who are weary or
doubtful or searching, with the eager among you and the
tentative and the hopeful, with you who are troubled or hassled
or blocked, with those of you thirsty for the waters of life and
those of you willing to travel once again the Emmaus-route. I
write with my family in mind, my sisters in community, friends
I have met along the way, young and not so young, in my own
country and in other countries, within my own church and
within the rich and responsive ecumenical community. Like
Habakkuk, it is time for me to write down my vision, so that
"others can easily read it". For even though the vision, yours
and mine, awaits its time, "it presses on to fulfilment, and it will
not disappoint" (Hab. 2:2-3).

Like all visions, mine is limited. By time and by my own
experience. Our human life and therefore our spiritual life

---

[2] All biblical references are from the *New American Bible*.

unfolds against our own histories and our cultural backgrounds. Only as we exchange discoveries and desires, share our questions and tentative conclusions, can the vision become common and useful. The words that rise within me and spill over onto these pages must meet an urgency in you, to gather the elements and to share *your* vision.

It is important that I acknowledge the debt I bear to certain people who have influenced my understanding of the Holy Spirit and who have led me into the implications of a life of exchange. One is John V. Taylor, whom I first met in *The Go-between God: the Holy Spirit and the Christian Mission.* So inspired was I by the vital interconnectedness his book describes that I immediately translated it into the work I was doing on my own community's rule of life. "The Holy Spirit", he writes, "is the invisible third party, who stands between me and the other, making us mutually aware."[3]

Implicit in the chapters that follow is an awareness of this role of the Spirit. Introducing us to the heart of another. Bridging for us our personal and larger worlds. Binding together our images into a comprehensive view of life and ministry. Leading us through the moments of search and the stages of our formation. Uniting our lives, in faith, to the words and deeds of the gospel. Gathering our obedience into the one will of God, who sent Jesus and now sends us. Setting us free, in the dynamic of love, to build an upside-down kingdom. Going between us and creation, opening our eyes and releasing our creative and life-giving forces.

Secondly, I am grateful to my Franciscan community that has nourished and guided me in my life of faith and in the meandering course of my ministry. At times they have been a home for me and at times a testing ground. They have encouraged my dreams and tolerated my comings and goings. They have freed me to pursue an ever-widening path of exchange, within the community itself, in global efforts for justice and peace, and in ecumenical sharing. Within that circle of international relationships and faithful friends, I learn something of the dailiness and the depths of discernment and discipleship. With them I recommit myself to the following of Francis and Clare.

---

[3] London, SCM Press Ltd, 1972, p.19.

The other person to whom I owe unlimited gratitude is not a formal author or a formal Franciscan. But Gwen Cashmore has introduced me to a *living* exchange, as my friend and fellow pilgrim. Our journey together in the last three years has taken us deep into faith and suffering and has borne us to the heights of joy and common vision. It has been an intercultural and an ecumenical journey. Its personal dimensions have been faithfully inserted into the context of the kingdom. Our life of exchange has convinced us both of its multidimensions and committed us to opening and enlarging that vision for others. In a very direct sense she has participated in the inspiration and gathering that have found their way into this book.

There is of course an inevitable and invisible go-between, the Holy Spirit, who dwells at the heart of this ongoing dialogue. "But what is this force which causes me to see in a way in which I have not seen? What makes a landscape or a person or an idea come to life for me and become a presence towards which I surrender myself? ... In every such encounter there has been an anonymous third party who makes the introduction, acts as a go-between, makes two beings aware of each other, sets up a current of communication between them."[4]

I call upon that force to open my eyes that I may recognize the creating, healing, probing hand of God in my life and in our world. I give thanks for the mysterious ways in which the "go-between God" has graced and transformed my own existence. And I pray that the communication and reflection engendered by this book may lead us all to invest more deeply in the cherishing and nurturing of our world.

---

[4] *Ibid.*, pp.16-17.

1. Life

"Polish people mourn kidnapped priest"
"South Africa's Bishop Tutu wins Nobel Peace Prize"
"Military leaders named in Aquino plot"

Bits and pieces of life. News headlines, moments of reflection. Glimpses of suffering and grief and hope. Stories of courage and the unconquerable human spirit. Fragments placed in our baskets with the day's scriptures. Nourishment and strength for the journey. Challenge and judgment as well.

All is sacrament

Moses was told: "Remove the sandals from your feet, for the place where you stand is holy ground" (Ex. 3:5). And holy also are the food you eat and the work you do and the people who work alongside you and your tired feet and that time of helpless horror called the evening news. All of it is sacrament. All intended to be noted and decoded and sanctified. All meant to alert us to the voice that speaks from the burning bush, or the blazing gunfire in Belfast or the burned-out building in Beirut. The voice that says: "I have witnessed the affliction of my people" (Ex. 3:7). I bid you read the cries and complaints of your world, ask questions, discover the meaning, and filter a bit of light and balm into its confusion and pain.

We are, all of us, spiritual beings inhabiting a spiritual world. All the human elements that make up our daily round of affairs: physical gifts and limitations, relationships, concerns and pet peeves, dreams, disappointments, mistakes, and claims to fame – all of these provide the material for our life of grace.

Spirituality embraces all of life, breathes through its homely details and its noble intentions. It is at the heart of our efforts to be human. It is the seamless robe worn in all our roles. Spirituality arouses in us an awe for the mystery of every human life. It is the lived connection of body and spirit, work and play, life and death. It is the reflection of our inner, honest, searching self and the expression of our tender, generous, hoping heart. It is the style of our judging and acting and the quality of our loving. It is the voice of our prayer and the progress of our pilgrimage towards peace. It is the silence of our struggles and the echo of our cry for justice. It is the ability to turn obstacles into opportunities and cacti into kingdom-signs. It is the truth of

1

our allegiances and the measure of our commitment to our world and its people. It is the scope of our wisdom, the test of our trust, the human translation of our Godlikeness. It is the realization that *every bush is burning*.

Perhaps most specifically, it is the degree of our harmony with all that is within and without us. We become spiritual when we inhabit our bodies, know our own souls, and insert ourselves gracefully into all that surrounds us. We become spiritual when we discern the sounds of our earth, recognize signs of pending destruction, speak the words of blessing and reconciliation. We become spiritual when we know ourselves as potential sisters and brothers of everything and everyone who has lived. We become spiritual when we find in this moment the message for today and in today the mission for tomorrow. When we experience the "in-one-ness" of life. Being spiritual demands the combined investment of our whole heart, our whole mind, our sexuality, our psyche, our sweat, and our very breath. "I came that they might have life and have it to the full" (John 10:10). Life fully human and fully spiritual, life integrated and incarnated.

As simple and concrete as bread

The story is told of Francis of Assisi and his companion Brother Masseo, who were journeying from town to town in France. As usual they begged for their food, Francis taking one street and Masseo another. Francis was small of stature and clearly a beggar and he earned only a few scraps of dry bread. But Brother Masseo was tall and handsome and he received large portions of fresh bread. They met outside the town near a fountain to share the alms they had been given. Masseo took note of what was lacking in their meal: cloth, knife, house, table, servants. But Francis could only exclaim joyfully: We are not worthy of this vast treasure. For we have bread, a table of stone, clear water, and God to serve us.

Perhaps spirituality rests in a point of view, the perspective from which we judge what is gift and what is burden. Perhaps this story of bread is a key to unlocking the spiritual depths of our hardened and ungrateful hearts. Bread, like rice in many parts of the world, is a basic symbol of life. Breaking bread is a ritual we all associate with Christianity. One simple gesture of bread broken and shared becomes universally symbolic of the life we share in Christ. We recognize the model, but we don't know, forcefully enough, our own position within that realm of sign and truth. Perhaps our use of bread, our sense of "living bread", our "in-one-ness" with bread, is a key to our spirituality.

In Milwaukee I belong to a worshipping community that endeavours to be clear about the meaning of bread. There are two events that prompt the community to come together, the eucharist on Sunday and the evening meal served daily below the church. Once a week a motley assembly lifts up bread and blesses it and distributes it, in memory of the life and death and continued life of Jesus. The poor are there and those who do not yet know how to become poor. The marginal are there: minorities, persons of other denominations, resigned priests, the homeless, alcoholics, the mentally disturbed. All are welcome and all are linked in a chain of solidarity as hands are joined and the Lord's Prayer sung. If anyone is uncomfortable at that table, it is those who are over-dressed, over-fed, and over-versed in liturgical rubrics.

Everyone at that celebration of bread comes to know the connection between the liturgy upstairs and the daily evening liturgy downstairs. When the doors open and the guests arrive, hospitality and friendship are served along with fish and bread. There may be five hundred on a given night. The cooks and servers may be young or old, black or white, sinner or redeemed, newcomer or old-timer. But the spirit is that of the eucharist: a community meal, a hospital atmosphere, the free gifts of God, and always enough for everyone.

This single illustration (though it is multiplied in many churches and in many parts of the world) may be sufficient for us to grasp the dynamics of spirituality. As simple and concrete as bread. As profound and as holy as the body of Christ. We are that body, however broken or out of touch we may be. And if we would realize our own identity and experience life more fully, we must feed one another. Those with more sharing with those who have little or none. Priests of the moment, offering the gifts of the earth and of our hands. A ceremony unfolding daily, not only on Sundays. We must be clear about what Jesus did and why, who he claimed as his own and for whom he laid down his life. We must be clear about our own community connections and the way we incorporate them into our deepest lifestream. Francis received life, and bread, as gift. The act of begging made that clear. The people of St Benedict's recognize the life that flows within the body of Christ, given faces and hands, in that State Street church. Each of us must touch and consecrate the bread made available to us. And enable the chain of life, the body of Christ, to grow.

In our inner cities in the US during these times, it is not unusual to see a figure bent over a trash can, rifling through the papers and debris, in search of a crust, an unwanted bite of donut. A sign of the decadence of our spirituality of bread. For even begging is not acceptable.

It is so easy to take bread for granted, to dismiss it even, in favour of richer, more cultivated foods. We have lost touch with the simple nourishment of simple folk. For many of us in the US bread appears in cellophane wrappers or in the form of frozen, ready-to-bake, loaves. A sign of the trivialization of our bread-culture. We have lost too the art of serving bread to one another. Intimate ceremonies of bread-taking, reminiscent of the eucharist and the exchange it entails, often deteriorate into fast eating in fast food places out of discardable containers.

And what would it mean for some of us to learn the mysteries of bread-baking, to experience bread as contour and smell and warmth? Might a generation of bread-bakers put us back in harmony with some of our roots, with something of the sacredness of our earth, its fields and harvest? Would it make us more mindful of hands and their capacity to shape and to create? Might it replace, as a sign of our hospitality and of celebration, the more costly and less nourishing offerings of snacks and hors d'oeuvres? Might we dare to serve one another bread, and with it, the possibility of a glimpse of God?

In choosing bread as a special sign of his presence in our midst, Jesus initiated a spirituality of ordinariness. Everyone understands bread. Its necessity for life. Its value as exchange. Its mystery of brokenness and death. The sign of union. In contrast to the banquets of the rich and the hoarded rations of the selfish. Bread for a hungry world. Agape bread. Symbol of reconciliation. Promise of the life and strength we are to become for one another. Francis led Masseo into the stream of spirituality that Jesus inaugurated at that one significant meal. Henceforth there were to be dimensions of the eucharist in every meal.

A spirituality of bread forces us also to examine the disobedience of our congregations and our churches when we deny bread to one another and excommunicate one another. Perhaps we disguise bread as wafers and fragments to make it easier for us to ignore what we are doing (and who we are excluding). In the breaking of bread and in offering it to one another, Christians remind themselves that they are the body of Christ. Irrevocably united despite doctrinal and denominational divisions.

Life is whole

What we have done or what we can succeed in doing with bread illustrates what we can do with all of God's gifts and with the spiritual life itself. Divorce it from its underlying nature as gift. Compartmentalize it and trivialize it so that we destroy its force and its transforming influence. Limit it to something "reserved", so that some people feel unworthy and others find it artificial and contrived.

There are ample signs in our world and in our somewhat empty hearts that this distortion of the spiritual life occurs. Often we are strangers to our inner life. We don't recognize its pulsings and reverberations. We practise spiritual exercises or indulge in worship services while we detach ourselves from our bodies and our physical surroundings. We keep matters of faith in one room of our life and we spend most of our time in the remaining rooms. We accept a lopsided and limited spirituality, narrowly focused on a one-dimensional God.

Serious consequences follow. Only parts of ourselves are drawn into prayer and the journey of faith. We leave behind, with a dogged sense of discipline, our senses, our imaginations, our creative impulses. We predetermine our places and times of prayer. We freeze our growth exactly where childhood instruction left us. We caricature God as a magician, a watchful parent, a bellhop, a capricious benefactor. We overlook the grace hidden in this practical event, this particular emotion, this here-and-now of beauty or pain or compassion. We read only the italics of our lives and neglect the common, everyday print. We use a language of the elite and fail to communicate the deeper dimensions of our lives to those around us. Our faith is clothed in mystique, our spiritual sharing is artificial, our vision of holiness becomes abstract and bloodless and unattractive. We approach life and people as problems. Mysteries are reserved to the Trinity. We trust computers and calculators but not our own healthy instincts and holy insights. We deprive our world of a sane and saintly approach to its problems and potential.

In our congregational life as well we begin to separate those who pray from those who act. We lose the vital connection between the repentance we articulate and the renewed efforts we practise outside the church doors. We divide our parish life into spiritual events and social and educational activities. We pray for the poor and the oppressed, but we can't locate Botswana or Haiti or identify with the plight of the Philippine islanders or the South Koreans. We discuss politics and go to films with Presbyterian and Methodist friends, but we've never been in their churches or understood their reticence to enter ours.

On a broader scale the law and order of our spirituality extend and apply to our social and national behaviour. When discrimination creates divisions, we legislate against sexism, racism, age-ism. We dare not acknowledge the seeds of the same in ourselves. We confuse defence with authentic security, so we are able to multiply our warheads and manufacture more technically sophisticated missiles. We foster an atmosphere of individualism, of pride in our achievements, and we value success, so that competition can continue. We allow the competition to spread from our private lives to our international relationships. We associate patriotism more with boundaries and battle-cries than with interdependence and international exchange. It is more important to be *first* than to be *friend*. Often we succeed in keeping our work and our play neatly categorized and carefully compartmentalized, also our loving and our sexual affairs, our business contacts and our friends, our social etiquette and our private behaviour. Life at all levels becomes a tightrope act of bridging dichotomies, balancing compromises, sustaining lost visions, and compensating for gnawing inner emptiness.

More and more we speak about and seek holistic medicine, healthier lifestyles, and friends who can read our music as well as our lyrics. We sense that life is meant to be whole and human, without deletions or censored spots. We gaze backward at the fervour of our first assignments and the enthusiasm of our former pastors. We suspect that sex has its own humour, that health includes peace of mind, and that the conversation late last night over wine was a holy event. We sympathize with our youth who resist being dragged to church. We search the poetry of Tagore and even the rock music of today looking for clues.

Perchance we stop long enough to study the stones thrown up by the waves or the fallen leaves cluttering our sidewalks. A new truth begins to emerge. Nature reveals to us what more nebulous theories of spirituality could not.

Nature is whole and each bit of nature is unique. The primrose that finds its way into the crevice of a cement stairway, and the awesome release of winter's wrath. Our world is polluted and violent and dying in many ways. But it is also etched with beauty and sharp with delicate detail. Francis knew the school of nature and recommended it to us. Praised be thou, my Lord, for brother sun, for sister moon, for our brother the wind, our little sister water, and for brother fire, for each is a gift and a sign. Each mirrors as no other the beauty and wisdom of God.

Life's own rhythms also become instructive. The natural rounds of sleeping and waking, growth and decay, maturing and ageing, silence and communication. Abstract truths and treatises on asceticism may tease our intellects and instill guilt in our unexercised wills. But we vividly grasp the meaning of renewal when we plough and plant a garden. And the paradoxes of our personality parallel those of eclipses and acorns and Indian summers. In the secrets of waterfalls and sand dollars and ancient trees we discover our own tangled histories and buried dreams.

We are not yet convinced that any place on earth can be holy: a city wall in Arles, a Jain temple in India, a hermitage on Mount Subasio, a street corner in Chicago. And that goodness and grace surround us: in the wheat we harvest, the letter we open, the sweater we knit, the child on our knee. We are sceptical still of the feasts of life, celebrated at this table with the people of this hour. We are hesitant to welcome the stranger and any inconvenient interruption. We barely notice that single star in our lonely night or the silent questioning eyes across the room. We fear to trust the intimacy and the energy of love. We yearn to be free from the dread of life, the sterility of our private enclosures, the paralysis of our guilt. We yearn to tell our stories, release our pent-up creativity, and reclaim our humanity.

We must dare to enflesh and incarnate our spiritual lives. To open ourselves to the hidden and the unexpected in our routine days and weeks. To become adept in penetrating life's meaning, and naming it. To believe in the newness and the naturalness of grace. To cherish our ordinariness and to encourage God to be bigger than ourselves.

We will begin to experience the sure and gentle touch of the Spirit, as our arid minds are watered, our wounded spirits healed, our numb hearts warmed and our rigid bodies made supple. Our prayer will be more spontaneous, our homes more hospitable, our concerns more global. Our work will be humanized, our personal powers tapped and our common wealth enhanced. Insignia and titles will be less important, our languages less limited, persons in remote places less foreign. Cancer might become a journey of hope, as we learn to harmonize our inner and outer environments. The US President and the Russians and the Curia in Rome will appear in our prayers as well as in our living room debates. Pentecost will be a time of bold undertakings in ecumenism. Meals will be more sacred and psalms more localized. The connections will be clearer between our small worlds and our large. We will begin to embrace our neighbour and our histories and our fragile planet. Our values and our creeds will become true in life as in word. Our name will be Christian and we will discover our family likeness.

The life we enjoy will spill over in our contacts and our contracts. We will be more aware of what we have in common: with the woman who aborted her baby, the young man facing draft registration, the unemployed coal-miner, and the less-than-inspiring priest. The gifts at our disposal will more easily find their way into others' hands: the once-read books crowded on our shelves, the large enough house to permit hospitality, the time it takes to tutor an immigrant or befriend a stranger, our bodily intervention at a scene of injustice. The products we buy will be seen in the context of the people who labour, the companies which discriminate and the waste we accumulate. Our hearts will be set in solidarity with the struggling migrant workers, the distant moulder of arts and crafts, and the deprived child of alcoholic parents. Together with those who beg their bread and those who distribute it, we will give thanks for our initiation into a world where nature and grace embrace.

At a meeting some months ago, a middle-aged woman, active and vibrant, challenged the participants to look alive and to live as if something excited them. I found myself thinking of a regular observation I make when I ride buses. Often I look at the sombre and silent faces around me, mannequins dressed up, propped up in their seats. Their eyes fixed on empty spaces, their hands crossed in resigned inertia. Are some of us dead already? It is a momentary brush with reality. And often a contrast to the faces I see that same evening on television. Intense and agonized. Desperate and determined. Protesting the assassination of their hero. Denouncing injustice and the evil of untruth. At moments like that I wonder: Is life something most of us evade, something to which we quietly resign ourselves? Or is life something to be grasped and defended? It has been entrusted to us to proclaim the word of life! What we have actively seen, what we have heard with discernment, what we have reverently touched. That is the life we announce to one another. That is the gift we offer, so that our common life may be enriched and enlarged. So that of the fullness of this life of the Spirit we may all have a share.

2. Search

The reign of God is like a buried treasure which someone found in a field. He hid it again, and rejoicing at his find went and sold all he had and bought that field (Matt. 13:44).

The story of human existence is shot full of the notion of treasure. Each of us as sojourners on this earth seeks that elusive and valuable gem called happiness, or the fulfilment of our dreams, or the kingdom of God. Not to search is not to be human. We are "homo viator", said Gabriel Marcel. We are people in search of meaning amid the sound and furies of our tortured, mad world. We are hollow men and women unless we have a quest to follow.

The human quest

The impulse to search is so strong that it has led human beings into the desert, into space, to the bottom of the ocean floor, and around the globe. People search for cures for modern diseases, for the secrets of the atom, for the most direct path to God. Ordinary folk search for the most satisfying career, the most reliable political party, the finest schools for their children, and the most nutritious diet.

Searching is an integral part of our education, though all too often emphasis is placed on answers rather than the quest itself. A whole segment of our academic endeavour is called research. Searching is part of our play: hide and seek, Easter egg and treasure hunts. We have been led to believe that searching hard enough and long enough will yield the desired results, whether they be the perfect vacation, the correct make-up, or the right marriage partner. Searching takes up a significant portion of our time and often becomes the very meaning of our short and limited lives.

Searching is also an integral part of our religious existence. Scripture provides us with numerous examples: the search for the promised land, the search for wisdom, the search for the lost sheep, the search to trap Jesus, Nicodemus's search for truth. Famous searches down through the centuries have been set before us, to inspire us, to console and encourage us. Monica's search for the soul of her son, Augustine's search for grace, the desert fathers, the founders and renewers of religious orders, the tested and the tried, the poets and the mystics, the reformers and the counter-reformers, the scholars and the missionaries.

Most of us come early in life to associate quest with the discovery of our personal vocation. Sadly enough our search often sinks into smug complacency after an initial choice, and we assume the truth of the course that follows. Until we are gripped by a particular sting of the flesh or crisis of faith, we often let up our search and lapse into careless and aimless wandering. Many are the drifters, not only among our adolescents, but among our adult and middle-aged population.

Does it sometimes occur to you that the greatest treasures are always in the depths? The treasure of the gospel is buried in a field. The pearl is buried in an oyster bed. Diamonds are hidden in crystallized forms far under the earth's surface. The limodore, the rarest of orchids, is hidden in the depths of the forest. The Carceri, a Franciscan hermitage, is hidden, like a jewel, in the deep foliage of Mount Subasio. New human life is entrusted nowhere but to the depths of a woman's womb. The secret of a human personality lies deep within the psyche. And the culture of a people is buried in the feats and the fathomings of their entire history.

Nothing worth knowing reveals its secret easily. Therefore only those who are serious and stout-hearted stand a chance to complete the quest. We must study the signs, break open the code, translate the message, pursue the footprints, wait upon the proper day and hour of revelation. This is true of the secrets of the spiritual life, the meaning of our dreams, and the place and expression of our personal response to the gospel. Like the treasure-seeker in the field, we must be prepared to dig and toil and persevere and wait. Each bit of ground must be uncovered and sifted for clues, if not for the actual treasure. We must be thorough and single-minded if we would not miss the tiny glimpse or the sudden movement or the unique sound of that which we seek.

The field in which we search is the space and time of your life and mine. And we are about the rhythm of planting and sowing, of ploughing under and of reaping. The process is sacred. The hope is always there, that with the seed and its silent growing, with the ploughing and its careful upturning, with the reaping and its multiple fruits, the treasure will slowly be revealed. Key to the success of the farmer and key to the progress of our spiritual journey is the task of ploughing. Unless the ground is broken into and overturned, there is no niche for the seed to root and sprout. Sharp prongs of the plough penetrate the firm and hardened earth, puncturing the stubborn clods and loosening the dry soil. So it is with the fields of our lives. A period of time, the ground of an experience, is broken open and shaken free. Reflection penetrates and pierces an event, so that its depths can be explored. The soil of our spirit is prepared for new seeds, new movements of grace, further action and further commitment. All the days of our life we plough with the farmer, furrow by furrow, field by field. Our apprenticeship in treasure-seeking.

Unlike the treasures of gold and precious gems, our treasure is less tangible. Regardless of our detours and our misconceived goals, we seek a treasure not of this world. We seek an elusive and spiritual goal, the kingdom of heaven. Only on that level are we offered an adequate exchange for our dearly-bought and slowly-gathered human treasures. Sell all that you have acquired, the young man of the gospel was told. Trade it in for a kingdom-treasure, solidarity with the poor. Then continue your quest. Trade in those possessions and those accumulated provisions for a life of trust and simplicity. Do it before you build your extra barns and before your life is taken by surprise. Invest your human gifts and talents wisely and daringly, so that you have treasure to exchange when the master returns. And trade in your sought-for places at the right and left hand of glory for the humble and obedient way of the cross. Such was Jesus' advice to James and John.

To recognize the kingdom-path we must be both wise and simple. In moments of wisdom and obedience, we come to realize that we are looking exactly in the wrong places and must take an upside-down position. The treasure is among the poor, not the powerful and prestigious. Among the pure of heart, not the sophisticated and knowledgeable. Among those who suffer persecution, not those who win approval and applause. We seek a treasure unaffected by time and unthreatened by thieves. We approach our treasure as our lives approach the outlines of the gospel. And finding it means we have lived out our deepest and truest vocation.

Every human vocation, each individual life, represents such a quest. We find in our particular and unique histories the fields we are to plough and harvest. You are a young evangelical searching for your own values and the best use of your musical talents. I am a Catholic Franciscan searching for the community with whom I can live my convictions regarding reflection, hospitality, and human exchange. Your neighbour is a native American, seeking employment and basic rights for his people. My nephew is an accountant, seeking to free his children of the worst of western consumerism and to invest his energies in a more credible political system.

In our own circumstances and out of our own resources, we gather the threads of meaning, discern the signs pointing us in new directions, and respond to the calls to go deeper and to walk more faithfully.

Reading our reality

Living a spiritual life means learning to read our histories, both private and common. We return to our sources: our childhood visions, moments of confirmation and conversion, our collected treasure of inspiring authors and fervent resolutions. We follow ourselves through relationships, job experiences, illnesses, surprises of one sort or another. We chart the breakthroughs and the betrayals, the awakenings to truth and the unmasking of our illusions. We locate ourselves and our particular moment of doubt or deliberation within the context of our family's crisis, our community's leadership, our church's efforts to dialogue with the world, global conditions of cold war and famine and unbalanced economies. We read the events that touch us this day: a papal visit to Switzerland, atrocities in El Salvador, the high rate of unemployment, the first rebellious signs in our adolescent daughter, our fear of the cancer that is killing a friend.

We read all these words of life and we seek their pattern. What is their message to us? Where are they calling us and what is the cost of following their clues? Which take priority, which fill us with anxiety, and which contain the map of the area of our treasure? We enter our days and our tasks with a constant question: Why do I do what I do? Why am I sorting papers on my desk, avoiding a report I must write, preparing for another week of meetings and another circle of evaluations? Why are you postponing that decision, denying your instincts, and calling it fate? Why do we fill our time with so many futile tasks and neglect the next plot of ground in our dearly-purchased field?

Our serious searching forces us to distinguish more clearly the essentials of our living from the expendables. We discover that absolutes can be relativized and fairy tales demythologized. Even when those absolutes revolve around family traditions or church discipline. And even when the myths include our self-images and our self-sustaining rationales. We bring to a halt our defence of ourselves and of our choices and we resolve to refrain from casting judgments on others. We rely on our life to be our testimony and we take steps to bring it into harmony with our proposed visions.

The gathering of threads, acuity in reading, facility in making connections, the ploughing under of our experience, are all part of our process of discernment. Alone and with others, we discern the way into obedience to the Spirit, into spiritual discipleship. Out of that movement further challenges arise and our metamorphosis continues.

Some of our searching calls us into the desert. The desert has always been a place of solitude and retreat, of the testing of one's spirit, of the discernment of our desires and our fears. Desert-dwelling enables us to shepherd our resources, to gain a perspective on the many and conflicting pressures of life, and to re-establish our relationships. In the desert we can listen more intently to the quieter voices speaking within our surrounding reality. We go apart, not to neglect others, but to learn how to meet them on more authentic levels. "Withdrawal from others", Merton suggests, "can be a special form of love for them... it may well be a quiet and humble refusal to accept the myths and fictions with which social life cannot help be full."[1] We come face to face with our exterior selves, begin to peel off our masks, and enter the possession of our truer selves. Finding that core is essential to embarking on a life of prayer and of exchange.

As "the Spirit scrutinizes all matters" (1 Cor. 2:10), so are we made attentive to the sounds and silences of our world. Our eyes are opened to the gift-quality of time and of opportunities and of

---

[1] Thomas Merton, *Disputed Questions*, New York, Farrar, Straus, 1960, p.192.

converging events. Occasionally we are shocked into this attentiveness. The launching of American missiles on European soil
alerts us to the groaning of the spirit in all of creation. The
sudden disappearance in the middle of New York City of a
young theology student horrifies us and plunges us into the
mystery of the life entrusted to our keeping. Our own words or
deeds move another human being further into grace and we are
humbled by the Spirit's prompting.

Our search also leaves in its wake a trail of efforts and
mistakes. We feel an inspiration, we embrace a particular
devotion or life-style, we engage in one cause or another in our
local and social life. Time reveals that we were misguided,
indulging our egos, out of touch with our limits. We recall the
wanderings of Jonah and Thomas the Twin and Mary Mag-
dalen.

A constant value of our community-living (and all of us live
in one or another kind of community) is the opportunity for
communal discernment. A tender story is told of Francis when
he faced the decision about the direction of his small company
of men and women. From his hermitage at the Carceri, Francis
pondered whether they should give themselves entirely to prayer
and contemplation, or whether they should also undertake the
preaching of the gospel. It was Francis' habit to ask advice of
others in discerning the will of God. So he sent a brother both to
Sister Clare and to Brother Sylvester, whom he clearly
respected, to ask them to pray and deliberate with him. Both of
them believed Francis was called to lead his companions into
the cities and towns, to an active apostolate, rather than form a
cloister, however necessary and good. When the brother
returned with the responses of Clare and Sylvester, Francis is
said to have asked: "What has my Lord Jesus Christ commanded
that I should do?" And immediately thereafter Francis left on a
preaching tour.

The basis for the religious vow of obedience lies within the
same experience. As a member of a community, we vow to
listen to the Spirit speaking within the members, and to commit
ourselves to follow that direction. The Spirit speaks in each
member of a community, a family, a congregation; the
youngest, the most radical, the slow to speak, the cynic, and the
most enlightened. We have hardly begun, I believe, to tap the

power and the wisdom of this spiritual resource. Too many of us are encrusted with individualism and unwilling to cast our trust and our futures into the hands of the Holy Spirit through this communitarian experience. What a gift we might offer our bewildered and groping world if we developed the art of discernment and gave witness to the fruit of such common searching and common sending! How much deeper might our interpretation be of the signs of our times! How much more concentrated our efforts to be a counter-sign in circles of avarice and violence! What a difference it might make if adopted by our scientific and defence industries and our international forums! When we are ready to forego the primacy of our own investments and agendas and accept the supremacy of the Spirit working within the combined insights of a particular community. When we believe that the Spirit can indeed create order out of our chaos and harmony out of our conflicts. When we are attuned to the surprises and the revelations that are Spirit-induced and that make our obedience a voyage of faith.

The inner search

Most of us would agree that there are elements in our society that manifest this unquenchable drive to follow a quest. One of the symptoms of our over-indulged, surfeited society in the West is the rebellion of some of our youth. Deliberate efforts to dissociate from the values and life-styles of their established and well-to-do elders. Sons and daughters of professional parents drifting across our countries and in and out of temporary jobs, to demonstrate their dissatisfaction with the status quo. Movements into communes, back to the earth, backpacking expeditions, natural food crazes, casual clothes, natural childbirth: all signs of a generation seeking new horizons and new rewards in life. Your parents may have boasted of their club memberships, pleasure boat, and company advancement. Their grandchildren are possibly prouder of their compost system, their summer peace camp, and their inter-racial friendships. Our churches have not particularly succeeded in attracting our youth. The young people are off to the Orient, seeking an ashram or a guru, or to the forest to commune with nature. Both the idealistic nature-lovers and those sweating it out in universities for the sake of better-paying and more secure careers are caught by a quest.

Another indication of western searching is the intense interest in self-understanding, psychological "togetherness", and therapies of all kinds. For some there are the simpler routes of journal-writing, communication techniques and workshops in assertiveness-training. Others opt for sensitivity sessions, psychotherapy, and the rigours of analysis. Bookstores are stocked with volumes that tantalize our inhibitions, correct our conditionings, and cater to our deflated or inflated egos, as the case may be. Groups are formed for the potential and actual alcoholic, drug-aholic, work-aholic, and even the food-aholic. It is not uncommon to find within the range of our acquaintances those who have had shock treatments or hypnosis, those who practise yoga and transcendental meditation, and those who find some solace in handwriting analysis or astrology.

There is a rash of interest in the inner life, the world of mystics and visionaries. Thomas Merton is still a popular author. *Siddhartha* is a bedside book, as are the fantasies of Richard Bach and the natural mysticism of Annie Dillard and the poetry of Dylan Thomas. People have taken to chanting mantras and the music of sea-sounds and animal-utterings. Gurus are part of our culture and there is a revival of interest in ascetic exercises, fasting, candle-light vigils, and prayer meetings.

Within our churches, women seek their just place and the laity seek leadership, and participation in decision-making. Protestants seek new understandings of spirituality and Roman Catholics seek greater ease with the scriptures. Churches of all denominations seek common forms of witness and face more honestly the search for a common eucharistic table. They search as well for new forms of missionary involvement and a more mutual sharing of gifts. Bishops seek to extend their authority and their credibility to areas of peace pronouncements and commentaries on economics and justice. Conversion rather than converts is emphasized and spiritual renewal rather than institutional growth.

In all of these movements and trends there is a common thread. A greater awareness of the relationship between our inner and outer worlds, between temporary achievements and lasting fulfilment, superficial satisfactions and qualitative peace. However distorted or fanatical the searches may become, there is within them a spiritual quality. In many, perhaps most, instances, there would be no conscious acknowledgment of the role and the impulse of the Holy Spirit. Yet it is within these natural leanings and these everyday interests that the Holy Spirit lurks, anonymous perhaps, unrecognized, and often uncelebrated. The Holy Spirit permeates the world of inner search, invisible light, unnoticed convergence.

Encountering the Spirit

Whether or not we are inclined to name the Spirit, we do encounter that mysterious force in concrete moments and specific exchanges. Especially those moments when we retreat to our own rooms and close the shutters of our daily distractions and disconnect the wires of claiming voices and pursuing demands. There we recover our inner selves, and in the space and silence of that refuge we experience the healing touch and the gentle affirmation of the spirit of solitude. We search for new styles of breathing and belonging.

In distinct moments of authentic encounter we meet the spirit of communion. Cradling the awesome miracle of a newborn baby. Looking into the eyes of someone who has just forgiven us. Looking through bars at the broken humanity of a woman dispossessed of her freedom. Reaching across an ocean to travel in spirit alongside a friend. Touching the tear-stained cheeks of a mother abandoned to her grief. Embracing with our hopes the just-wedded couple. Recognizing the fear and the pain in the faces of a newspaper photo. Holding in our helplessness the victims of an earthquake in Turkey. In the profound stirring of those encounters we experience the spirit of compassion and gentleness and reverence for life. We search for understanding and a deeper sense of our human relatedness.

In periods of agonizing and endless waiting we meet the spirit of unremitting hope. A sleepless night, enduring the slow tick of time, anxious about the burden of our illness or our alienation. Vigils, commemorating the horrors of Hiroshima, protesting the electrocution of a human being, awaiting the outcome of a serious operation. More than sentinels wait for the dawn, our spirits wait for the lifting of darkness and the assurance of a new day. And periods also of innocent and childlike waiting. The coming of summer, our day of commencement, the advent of a long-awaited friend, the arrival of a letter, of a plane, of a new member of the family. We are like Samuel in our naive ignorance of the significance of the event. In the ordinariness and anticipation of those moments we encounter the spirit of renewal and of purifying patience. And later realize the difference our waiting made and its fruitfulness for ourselves and for others.

In times of decision-making and difficult choices we meet the spirit of faith. The direction of our lives. The sealing or surrendering of a relationship. A conscience matter, a principle that cannot be betrayed. The how and when of our solidarity with the poor and oppressed. Our response to a bitter assignment. A conviction lived out amid rejection and hostility. "In your plans for us there is none to equal you" (Ps. 40:6). In the tearing temptations and frightening implications of those moments we encounter the spirit of fortitude and stability and truth. And we are grateful for the grace poured out on us by the Spirit who governs such affairs for the weak and the willing.

In moments of total unawareness and even actual evasion we meet the spirit of forgiveness. Lectures and films and first-hand experiences laid aside and forgotten. Routine, mechanical trips to church and to relatives and to the sites of our ministry. Letters unanswered and invitations rejected. Signs misread and flowers unsmelled and little people neglected. Wasted grace and discarded gifts. We are like the miner searching for gold and throwing out the ore, the farmer harvesting crops and casting aside the roots of carrot and potato. "I have seen the sun break through to illuminate a small field for a while, and gone my way and forgotten it."[2] Or we isolate ourselves in self-pity and resentment. Proclaiming ourselves victims of life and its catastrophes. Hoarding our valuables and locking up our talents and insights. Escaping scenes of despair and ugliness. Refusing responsibility for the effects of our choices. Determined to thwart the disarming tactics of the spirit of mercy and tolerance and perseverance. And encountering in our shuffling and our dodging the eternal hound of heaven. "More tortuous than all else is the human heart... who can understand it? I, the Lord, alone probe the mind and test the heart..." (Jer. 17:9-10).

---

[2] R.S. Thomas, *Later Poems*, London, Macmillan, 1983, p.81.

The Holy Spirit does not force an entrance into our crowded lives and our cluttered consciousness. The Holy Spirit does not reward our searching with instant or spectacular results. Rather, the Spirit waits for a vulnerable moment, a sign of recognition, a cracked rim on our closed hearts, and slips in, to prompt out of a tragedy a time of conversion, out of a casual event a miracle of grace. The Spirit turns an empty space into a treasure trove and a searcher into a gleaner of secrets. The Spirit is a companion in all our searches, a guide, and a director. If we will but allow room and open ourselves to the transforming influence of this unobtrusive guest.

Our failure to search

There are those of us who, in our journey through life, would like to forego search. We are impatient with the unknown and the partially clear and the delays. We prefer to arrive at our destinations as quickly as possible and we are incapable of enjoying the journey itself. We are interested in results, rather than process, in the attaining of our goals rather than the effects on our lives of detours and unexpected happenings. We are opportunists, uncomfortable with leisure, irritated by tardy responses, and abhorrent of any form of laziness. We transfer these needs and notions to our larger society. If a first marriage is not successful, we attempt a second or a third. If life offers more problems than we can cope with, we engage a therapist and expect a cure in three months' time. If we can't find the assistant or the partner we fancy, we advertize in the newspaper, or put the information on a computer.

In the US we propel our cars onto freeways whether or not there is room for them. Follow the leader day after day, twice a day, in our commuterized processions. Fast-food restaurants, instant printing, drive-in banking, dial-a-prayer, help remove any possible search or delay in our modern, sophisticated milieu. Our children learn rapidly to expect that "I want" will be followed by "I get". And they follow adults in dashing from one exciting experience to another, planning the next excursion before the previous one has been paid for. We develop an "as we go" mentality. We will pollute our cities and our rivers today and worry about the air and the fish tomorrow. We will build dangerous weapons systems while we have public support and leave it to future generations to discover how to rid the world of nuclear waste. We will buy the new stereo or sports car this month and face the payments on the first of many months. We will indulge and ignore our health today, for tomorrow we may indeed be confronted with lung cancer or heart disease. We will borrow time or steal it for our favourite sport or hobby, but we will reluctantly take time to examine our values or the reasons for our disquietude and our boredom. More and more we confuse the treasure we seek with the treasury of our accounts and the amassing of our assets.

Over and over again we become the victims of our failure to search and our inability to plough under our experience. We fail personally and we fail as a people. In the US we were slow to learn the lessons of Vietnam and so we blunder in Lebanon and repeat our stained history in the countries of Latin America. It is easier to shore up the economy with newer and more costly defence products than to take the creative and long-range course of conversion of our defence industries. For many of our churches it is less risky to suppress women than to rethink their participation and their roles in ministry. Our patterns of relating as nation to nation, our diplomacy, and our summit meetings, our conflicts and our cold wars, are identified with our survival and our supremacies, and we dare not envision the possibility of living as a united and interdependent world.

Our lives are linked

Discernment in our society is desperately lacking. The combined wisdom of human minds and the courage and conviction of human hearts discerning the directions of medical science: human embryos, transplants, machine-induced survival. The just distribution of resources, so that crops need not be destroyed in one country while innocent families starve and suffer malnourishment in other regions of the world. Perhaps discernment is most clearly and crucially needed regarding the future of the planet earth itself. We are all caught in a tornado-like spiral of fear and dread and unimaginable destruction. Some of us choose to ignore the nuclear threat and live our lives on a day-to-day basis, worried about our taxes and the vandalism in our neighbourhood. Don't suggest that our taxes enable the arms race to escalate and that violence is a spectrum reaching from the disfigurement of our public buildings to the destruction of mother earth. Some of us choose to believe that war and militarism are inevitable realities, and that it is simply better to support a system that allows us individual freedom than one which curtails private pursuits. Don't suggest that freedom and private pursuits are limited goals when a cloud of fear hangs overhead, threatening to obliterate us and all that we enjoy and all that we covet.

Some of us want to discern how to live in a nuclear age, how to influence those who make life and death decisions for us all. How to raise children in a world that seems doomed to explode. How to be responsible for the gift of life now and for the preservation of life on earth. No one of us today, it would seem, can separate our inner search, our personal vocation, from the surrounding and encompassing reality of weapons and their use. Our search must include a search for peace, peace at all levels, peace rooted in justice, peace for all. Small groups around the world, communities, networks, attempt this kind of discernment. We must find our way into such a circle, contribute our insights and our efforts and our sacrifices. Our lives are linked, Europe and Asia, North America and Africa, South America and the Pacific. Our fields border one another and our treasures are trivial when taken out of the context of our life in common and our common destiny. Peace is not an issue to be researched, nor entrusted solely to those who are professed pacifists. A living, witnessing search for peace is our responsibility. Not to be alert to the levels of peace-making and related facets of reconciliation is to deny a spiritual dimension of our personal quests and private relationships. Through constancy in discernment we must help shape our future, not merely react to the negative forces about us.

In this area and in others our society is yearning for a new kind of leadership. Many people in our western nations have lost faith in the political process and in the genre of leader it produces. In the US an appalling percentage of eligible voters do not bother to cast their ballot. In the eyes of many there is so little difference between candidates of opposing parties. It seems that all have been coopted by the inevitable demands of bureaucracy, by big business or big labour unions, and have lost touch with the common folk and the issues that affect them.

Where are the charismatic leaders, the emergence of a new cadre of women and minorities? Where are the bold and the free and those willing to risk their political futures in enfleshing their own convictions?

We search as well among the candidates for church offices for the spiritual leader who is eager to make visible the unity the office symbolizes, willing to initiate in his or her own life the principles of simplicity and solidarity and a dynamic spirituality. Many Christians are weary of church administrators and eloquent scholarship. They hunger for the nourishment of a gospel made relevant, and a liturgy which includes them and in which the reality of a common meal is recognizable.

More of us are less enamoured with the person who covets positions of leadership, who becomes unavailable once elected, and who gradually succumbs to compromise and caution. Where are the gentle spirits and the prayerful souls among our leaders? When will we trust the qualifications of credible life-style and courageous witness as much as articulation of programmes and financial expertise? When will we die to the styles of government and authority that characterize our secular society and choose the style of the gospel? So that what is most evident in those who direct and encourage us is their pilgrim status, their ability to listen and to learn and to change, and their global sensitivity. Persons who can share their own spiritual adventure and who release and affirm others to do the same.

Such leadership of course is dependent on the willingness of all of us to become this kind of salt and leaven in our various communities and confessions. Dependent also on our willingness to trade in a degree of efficiency and solvency, an image perhaps of professionalism or organizational faultlessness. And to support and summon the humbler and more prophetic in our midst to accept the role of guide and shepherd.

As we discern and create our personal and shared worlds, we can actually sometimes name the search we are making. We stand back, do some map reading, assess our direction. And we see something that evaded us in the isolated moments and the thick of our activities. As I stand back at this point in my life, I recognize the threads of a search that has extended from my earliest years of adulthood to the present. In my choice of entering a religious community there was a blurred, but real, desire to bring life to others as I discovered a life within. In retrospect, I can see that each time my life became overcrowded and over-complicated, there surfaced in me a clear desire to go apart and to rediscover the inner way. At one point in the midst of my doctoral studies, overwhelmed and disturbed by their headiness and esoteric quality, I thought I heard a contemplative call. Leave all these abstractions and join a more cloistered community. At another crucial time, over-invested and over-extended in efforts for peace and justice, my health broke, and I was forced to slow down and take time to reflect and evaluate. The major crossroads in the last twenty-five years of my life have been choices to enlarge or diminish the active and reflective sides of my ministry. The search is for a balance. But a balance that fits my contemporary world and its blatant cries as well as my personal make-up, my gifts and my limits. There have been difficult moments when I couldn't explain myself to others, my change of direction, my sudden stops, partly because I didn't understand myself. There seemed to be an inner guide directing me, however, a sense of my own rhythms and the lines of continuity. As I stand at my present vantage point, I see a weaving of the elements of activity and contemplation and I see the central path that has not been broken, a way to live in relation to and in exchange with the larger world, at the same time guarding and ensuring a life of reflection and of solitude.

The new moment in my search is that I long to do that more clearly and more visibly with others. I long to discern that way, that kind of presence in our world, with a community with similar yearnings. I long for companions on my journey, a journey of holding in balance involvement and prayer, responsible action and searching reflection, the call to go abroad and the call to go deep. At this point as in the past, I do not know the next bend in the road, the next signpost, the next stop-over. I believe the journey is worth making, the revelations will come, the way will unfold. In some mysterious way I understand, through my own search and my own wanderings, the meaning of the forty years in the desert, the Exodus experience, Jesus' trips to the mountain tops, the journey to Emmaus.

I want to build with others a bit of the kingdom in the remaining years of my life. Again and again my companions and I have recognized Jesus on the way, have had the scriptures interpreted to us, have felt our hearts burning within us. We know that in each breaking of the bread in the company of other believers, and in the daily journey into the Galilee of our lives, our quest resumes.

Each of us seeks a treasure. It is elusive and difficult to achieve. It attracts us even when we aren't sure of its contents. The longing for it sustains us on rough and dangerous terrain. In the searching we already possess the sought-for. We journey all the days of our lives, with hope in our hearts, led by the Spirit. One day there dawns the realization that we must give all we possess in exchange for the pearl of great price. In the end, the one "who searches hearts" knows our spirit and our intention, and it is God's glory that is revealed in us.

3. Formation

One day a farmer went out sowing. Part of what he sowed landed on a footpath, where birds came and ate it up. Part of it fell on rocky ground where it had little soil. It sprouted at once since the soil had no depth, but when the sun rose and scorched it, it began to wither for lack of roots. Again, part of the seed fell among thorns, which grew up and choked it. Part of it, finally, landed on good soil and yielded grain a hundred- or sixty- or thirtyfold (Matt. 13:4-9).

We spoke earlier of bread, as an image of life and as a clue to our spiritual awareness. We speak now of seeds and of sowing. Of soils and their capacity for new life. We speak of spiritual formation.

Jeremiah's image of forming is that of the potter. "I went down to the potter's house and there he was working at the wheel. Whenever the object of clay which he was making turned out badly in his hand, he tried again, making of the clay another object of whatever sort he pleased..." (Jer. 18:3-4). And the message to the Israelites in exile was: "Like clay in the hand of the potter, so are you in my hand, house of Israel" (Jer. 18:6).

Ignatius of Loyola saw formation in terms of fitness, as spiritual exercises. Perhaps it was the consequence of his earlier career as a soldier. The exercises entailed self-scrutiny, careful use of the imagination, and the training of the will. The object was to prepare the spiritual trainee to choose a new way of life.

Francis of Assisi described his own formation in terms of a single radical act. His initial contact with Lady Poverty was a transforming event. Francis had a horror of lepers. But one day he couldn't escape, or chose not to. He met one face to face. And he submitted himself to that forming encounter. Francis embraced the leper and kissed him. Fear died and conviction was born. Poverty was to be henceforth his school and his rule of life.

Influenced by society
Our western society is keenly conscious of the process of formation. "Socialization" rather than the spiritual life is the object. Let us not underestimate the care and resources invested in this process by some of our most astute planners. Our political chiefs know that a patriot is formed by constant

propaganda and manipulative appeals to loyalty and sacrifice. I dare say we hear more about sacrifice these days from our governments than from our churches. Our business leaders and company presidents calculate with amazing accuracy the influence that the media and its advertisements have on the life-style and choices of the consumer. The medical establishment relies on its incomprehensible jargon and its mysterious diagnostic tests to form its passive and compliant clients. Our sense of fashion is formed by models and film stars and by what the rich can afford. Children are formed by their toys, as little girls imitate their elders with cosmetic kits and little boys with Star War games. The object of education, if analyzed, is more likely to be social conformity or job fitness than critical thinking and global awareness. We imbibe the values of our culture from our cereal boxes and our soap operas more readily than from our philosophers or moral theologians. More is better, our billboards assert, and waste is normal. Speed and efficiency are marks of progress and only the quaint and the disabled continue their craftwork. Shopping centres compete with churches for Sunday attendance. Sex is sold in magazines and theatres and via multiple products for enhancing and encouraging promiscuity. Interest in sports is almost patriotic, and baseball heroes are always included among the "ten most admired men".

All around us signs and slogans and significant personalities advise us in our grooming and our purchasing and our vacationing. Package-deals and instant results and latest models lure us into our society's insidious snares and sins. Resisting this formation is not only difficult, it is suspect. Economy becomes confused with civics. And conscience is secondary to national pride. We face a jungle of appeals in our personal and family life. And often find ourselves in a desert of spirituality, where guidance is less available, road-signs less clear, and where expertise and example become ever more scarce.

There is another dimension to this societal formation. From patterns of fear or the pain of experience, we double-lock our doors and neglect our neighbours. We avoid certain sections of our cities and check our rear-view mirrors for would-be pursuers. Good Samaritan acts sometimes backfire and are so rare that they merit newspaper coverage. Spontaneous conversations on streets or buses are mistrusted. And we dare not catch the eye of the driver who waits next to us at the stop light!

Beating the system and stealing from our employment places are acceptable and often lauded. Our prisons are inhabited by the poor and by social outcasts rather than by those who perpetrate untruth and injustice. The countries of our world are labelled friend or foe (and our own citizens red or rednecked) and the labels change according to expediency. Many of us would prefer not to be disturbed by stories of Africa's famine. We manage to maintain the boundaries of colour and class. The politics of fear permeates our political campaigns so that voices of renewal and hope are judged naive and irresponsible. More out of principle than necessity we compete for jobs and for status and for nuclear superiority. We multiply the economic and political barriers that divide us and lose our faith in the possibility of common efforts for a united world.

The seeds of growth

No wonder the words of Ezekiel intimidate us: "I will give you a new heart and place a new spirit within you, taking from your bodies your stony hearts and giving you natural hearts" (Ezek. 36:26). And we squirm uncomfortably at Paul's challenge to the Ephesians: "You must lay aside your former way of life and the old self which deteriorates through illusion and desire, and acquire a fresh, spiritual way of thinking" (Eph. 4:22). In the quieter corners of our crowded hearts we realize the gap between our faith and our faithless compromises, our spiritual calling and our comfortable conditioning. We turn a small corner and take up again the life-task of our spiritual formation.

For that is precisely how our spiritual growth occurs, gradually, with attention and effort, step by step, through lapses and conversions, long pauses and occasional leaps. An ongoing process through which we become oriented to our Christian vocation. A process that depends on our awareness of the factors which impinge on our freedom and our steadfastness. The transformation takes place within – "true circumcision is of the heart" (Rom. 2:29). All that engages us and every human situation are potential formation experiences. Our response determines their long-range value. We experience periods of slow, imperceptible growth as well as times when we are formed more radically. We plunge ourselves into the ordinary dough of life and, guided by faith, we knead our spiritual selves. We receive the seed of a gospel vision and we struggle to produce a lasting fruit.

When the underlying meaning of an event is opened to us, and we discover that the message has a personal implication, we face a moment of formation. The situation in which we find ourselves stirs our faith. A spark leaps up, together with new energy and new light. The closer we are to life, in its vivid and explicit manifestations, the more invested we are in our relationships and our socio-historical milieu, the more possibility there is that our faith is quickened. Much more than theories or sermons, experiences transform and convince us. And rather than words or rewards, the living example of others motivates us.

When virtue becomes concrete, and ideals are made specific, we are more apt to see the spiritual implications. Grasped by the experience, we emerge more aware, more sensitive, more focused, more impelled to new behaviour. The whole range of human experience and encounter is available, as the setting for conversion and renewal. Moments of trial, of challenge, of reflection, of tenderness. Scenes of pain and brutality and confusion. Times of waiting, of decision-making, of tranquillity.

My novice director had a favourite saying. As the twig is bent, so the tree is formed. It was her starting point for encouraging us to practise assiduously the spiritual habits that she inculcated. Our novitiate was a nursery and we were admittedly hot-house plants. We were growing in the most protected of environments. Select conditions for rooting and sprouting and budding. Opportunities for sacrifice and mortification. Supervised curtailing of our appetites. Constant reminders of the way to holiness: lives of saints, feats of our foundresses, models of asceticism. But it would not always be so, she warned us. We would be forced to transplant ourselves one day into a complex world full of distractions and temptations. How easy it would be to stunt and distort our spiritual growth! How important it was to be grounded in behaviour that would resist the cold winds and the heavy frosts of life outside the nursery.

The image of the tree is still a favourite of mine, but now it emerges from Psalm 1: "She is like a tree planted near running water, that yields its fruit in due season, and whose leaves never fade" (v.3). For most of us, there is no protected time and place of formation. Hot-houses for the young and aspiring are not particularly part of our spiritual pedagogy. That one spiritual giant called the novice director no longer exists. Nor do we have the benefit of her uncanny knowledge of our exact progress in absorbing virtue and avoiding vice. A variety of influences has replaced her and much more responsibility is handed us for choosing our soil and measuring our growth. But each of us, whatever our chronological and spiritual age, is a composite of tender shoots and struggling saplings. We aim to grow up to our full spiritual stature, to become this ever-green, ever-fruitful tree. We recognize the distinctive pressures of climate and weather. We accept that our fragile tendrils must be exposed to all seasons and all conditions. And that our naive and eager hearts must undergo pruning if they are to be the new and natural hearts Ezekiel describes.

The very atmosphere around us forces some formation upon us. It happens before we are critically aware of spiritual means and spiritual goals. So often now in my adult life I recall a scene or a saying of my mother and realize they have influenced the person I now am. The image of my mother housing and feeding an elderly man, without family and without means. Even tending his gangrenous leg. My recollections of Lenten rosaries prayed after supper around the kitchen table, against the background of a coveted neighbourhood ball game. Indelible pictures of my invalid mother, subjected to complete dependency, patiently accepting our awkward assistance. Seeds she bequeathed to me of hospitality and discipline and fortitude in suffering.

The Vietnam War played a crucial part in the formation of my social consciousness. Once I allowed the Vietnamese people and the horrors inflicted upon them to enter my consciousness and my conscience, I found myself changing. Through the person and stories of To Thi Anh, I met my Vietnamese sisters and their lives were inextricably woven with mine. It was the beginning of my search for information, for solidarity with others concerned, and for ways of responding to travesties of peace and justice. I found my way from letter-writing and group rallies to public prayer vigils and a public fast. No longer could I force that world of napalmed bodies and courageous spirits into the background of my mind. Nor would I know integrity until I had embraced a portion of their struggle.

I lived alone for a period of time. A two-room apartment, modest but comfortable. I made my own decisions, followed my own schedule, handled my own budget. I parcelled out my time and my availability to others. I revelled in the solitude and in the joy of styling my own life. And very quickly I learned the wisdom of community and shared living. The latter brings more clearly to light our motives for certain laudable acts. Do I pray regularly or do I pray to be seen? Do I live simply, out of principle? Shared living demands a truth and a generosity that can be stifled in a solitary environment. The value of my time-allotments. My fidelity in deed to the promises I profess. The balance of exchange and of privacy. Life in community is a safeguard against individualism and selfishness. It prevents us from rationalizing and calls us to name our deviations and discern our directions.

It is in the interplay of our lives with life around us that our growth is nurtured and our blossoms yield fruit. The choices we make are at the very heart of this process. The choices whereby we insert ourselves into our world with its human frailties and its indomitable spirit. Or the choices whereby we protect ourselves from its harshness and its demands. The books we read, the people we allow to inspire and guide us, the countries we visit and the manner in which we visit them, the work we do and the kind of world our work creates, the information we take in and the tests we give it, the communities with which we network and the concerns we share. Or the opportunities we bypass: the Advent retreat, the call to exercise leadership, the plight of a neighbour, the new skill or a new language, a necessary confrontation, a moment of truth. Out of these choices we shape the contours and the capacity of our spirits. We learn the importance of spiritual nourishment and the meaning of the gospel bidding: "They are about to faint from hunger; give them something to eat yourselves" (Mark 6:37).

Come and see

To the first disciples Jesus said: You would know me, understand my life, begin a formation experience. Then you must "come and see", engage yourself in my activities, taste the life you aspire to follow. Learn the ingredients that will transform your vision and your values. Encounter the paradoxes that will enable you to see differently, to rearrange your priorities, to recognize the signs of my kingdom. And become the soil that yields a hundredfold.

We "come and see" that it is in giving that we receive. For three months I gave India my full attention, all my energies, and my best spiritual insights. But India gave me, in addition to her culture and her beauty, a vision of faith in following a mission, of hope in facing tremendous obstacles, and of joy in celebrating the simple gifts of life. In that exchange of gifts, I was fashioned into a new clay pot, into new soil. I was tested in my willingness to be shaped by another culture. And probed until my deepest inner resources were exhausted and then replenished.

We "come and see" that it is in pardoning that we are pardoned. A friend told me her reactions during a recent experience. Great Britain and Argentina were fighting their war in the Falklands. My friend, who is British, found herself at a meeting with a musician from Argentina. Both felt a strong sense of sadness and of solidarity as the war was discussed. Their embrace was a redeeming act in an unredeemed war. So many of our historical sins remain unredeemed. Forgiveness has not been asked and pardon has not been given, and the wounds continue their rankling. Americans still carry Pearl Harbour into encounters with Japanese. Who of us can fully forgive the Nazis? And how long before the Russians will ask forgiveness of the South Koreans for the lives lost on Flight 007? All of us have still to be formed to pardon and repentance. We have not yet imbibed: "Father, forgive them for they know not what they do" (Luke 23:34).

It is even more difficult to "come and see" that it is in dying that we are born to eternal life. It has been the message of hope in the witness of saints through the centuries, in the martyrdom in our own day of Dietrich Bonhoeffer, Edith Stein, Martin Luther King, and Oscar Romero. And the ray of light in the lives of the mothers of Argentina, the mourners of the Lebanon massacres, and the survivors of every battle and every catastrophe. It is the reflection of every group that flanks a grave site and a piercing reminder as we read news headlines. Learning to let go, to give up something or someone precious, to lay down our lives, is the theme of our Christian formation. And step by step we penetrate the truth and the freedom of this paradox. "Unless the grain of wheat falls to the earth and dies, it remains just a grain of wheat. But if it dies, it produces much fruit" (John 12:24).

We come to see as well that formation happens more readily and more effectively within a framework of belonging and acceptance. It is our rootedness in our families and our churches that enables us to seek and welcome renewal. It was the rootedness of the prodigal son in his father's love and acceptance that enabled him to recognize his errors and to return to his vocation as son. The rootedness of Ruth in the affection of her mother-in-law enabled her to give up the familiar for life in a foreign land. Rooted in various traditions of worship and spirituality, the delegates at the Vancouver Assembly of the World Council of Churches could be embraced by a common Spirit as they prayed in each other's tongues. With deep roots in Christianity and Hinduism, an ecumenical ashram can explore the riches of both. Our transformation occurs against the backdrop of a secure and trusting community. When we know to whom we belong, we can dare to challenge that very foundation and to renew our traditions and charisms. Experiences of intimacy free us to delve deeper into our motives, to extend ourselves further in ministry, and to aspire beyond our current levels of commitment. "Anyone who loves me will be true to my word... we will come and make our dwelling place with such a person" (John 14:23). How difficult, by contrast, to venture into the unknown and to risk failure and defeat when one is not sent, not supported, and not sure of a return reception.

Coming and seeing involves practical day-by-day participation. One learns to pray by praying. One becomes a community-person by unflagging efforts to adapt and to understand. One learns compassion by on-the-site discoveries of human need and response. One thinks globally by dieting steadily on sifted information and critical reflection. Life's experiences, if entered and not dodged, lived and not avoided, render us vulnerable, open our sensitivities. We enter our hospital wards, our prisons, our city halls, and our skid rows, and we may lose some of our prejudices. We study our educational systems, our environment, our relations with second and third world countries, and our life-styles begin to be converted. We grapple with systems and structures and stereotypes, and we begin to insist that we and others be treated as persons, not as social security recipients or delinquents or refugees. We not only serve the meal at St Benedict's, we sit down next to the stranger and partake of a common table. We begin to register our helpless feelings and to pool them in planning and in prayer. We allow the day's burdens and bereavements to flow into tears and into firmer bonds with those who have shared them. To qualify as ministers of healing and wholeness, we cannot be strangers to the gripping clutches of psychic and physical pain. Rather, we must allow the shocks and stark realities to form us into "wounded healers".

Necessarily our coming and seeing stretches us out of our inertia and complacency. Nothing was so revealing to me of my complacent attitude towards "foreigners" than my journey to India. For foreigners had always been the "others". I was always at home. Suddenly curious eyes followed my western dress, I felt paranoid in the midst of Malayalam or Hindi voices, and buses and city streets threatened me with their crowds and beggars and random jostling. I reacted to the slow and seemingly discourteous treatment at the airport. I was impatient with the bureaucracy and the endless queues and the total lack of punctuality. It was necessary for me to become a foreigner before I could cross over into an understanding and empathy.

Each time we cross over to the unfamiliar, we catch a glimpse of a bigger and more complete world. Until then, we are able to think we can get along without each other. We might judge others to be ungrateful and inferior. Once we cross over into others' worlds and view their treasures and walk their terrains, our attitudes and awarenesses change. We cross over as well into the beauties of antiquity, the perspective of another culture, the familiarity of an Indian peasant with earth and sky. Those enclosed in narrow worlds continue to discriminate with jokes and distort the facts about another race, another denomination, another life-style. They have not held their victims' babies, received their benedictions, understood their protests.

For some of us, the experience of stretching begins in our own cities: meeting our neighbours, using a laundromat, attending a store-front service. I have never actually lived among the poor, sharing their plumbing and their cockroaches and their sub-standard medical treatment. As a result, my sense of justice is still somewhat dulled and side-tracked into more middle-class issues. My values of silence and solitude (privacy perhaps) are also protections and luxuries. My notions of hospitality and trust are limited and represent a minimal risk. I rejoice in the crossing over that India represented, that friends in other countries facilitate, that my association with the World Council of Churches has fostered and developed. For each of us there is a realm of untasted life. Customs and beliefs and ceremonies that would make our lives richer and more fully human. We have a long way to go, as people, as churches, as countries, in recognizing our true identity and our spiritual heritage, the wealth of our diversity and the strength of our unity. We can only encourage one another to cross over, into music and art, and worship, and stories of struggle and liberation.

I pose three particular areas in our contemporary life that call for "a fresh, spiritual way of thinking". They form an agenda for us personally, denominationally, and as citizens of our world. They demand our attention if we would be spiritually mature and catalysts for the growth of others.

Learning silence

I believe we need to be formed into people of silence and contemplation. To become soil which the Spirit can penetrate and impregnate. A title of an article once caught my attention: "The greatest scarcity of our times". The next line revealed that silence was the resource in question, the commodity hard to come by. Words fill up so much of our day. Conversations rarely yield to silence. We fill up our time, otherwise unmapped, with the sound of television or phonograph. We switch on the car radio immediately after the ignition. We substitute all too often more words for deeper thought. We honour those who are articulate and we take courses in speech and debate. At work we are surrounded by ringing phones and the steady hum of motors and machines. Our recreations are punctuated by loud music, human voices, and traffic sounds.

Silence is often uncomfortable, whether in the company of others, or at a time of prayer. We prefer hymns and readings to quiet meditation. A thirty-second pause for reflection finds us day-dreaming and planning tomorrow's menu. And causes some to think the leader lost the page. Persons with a contemplative bent are a bit eccentric. We even attempt to measure the products and fruits of our prayer.

Sometimes we do sense that our pace is too frenzied, our hearts and minds too cluttered, and our lives too dissipated. We long for the space and time of a free weekend or a holiday. Until one or the other comes and we pitch into them, full force, crossing off our lists, catching up on sundry tasks, and assuaging our guilt with visits and returned hospitality. Perchance an unexpected illness slows us down enough to take stock of our busy lives and our relatively empty spiritual coffers. Or retirement suddenly faces us and we are unprepared for its loneliness and our seeming uselessness.

What will facilitate a practice and a priority of solitude and reflection? For surely silence is of the Spirit. And the gospel frowns on one who prays to be noticed and who "rattles on" like a "noisy, clanging cymbal". Wisdom is born of silence and meditation. Presence, to another person, to the situation at hand, demands a perceptive eye and a listening ear. Our choices and finest plans and projects are conceived and nurtured in the womb of a prayerful, discerning heart. Reflective moments purify and redirect our impulsive actions.

Putting ourselves in relationship is the key to our entrance into solitude, into shared silence, into creative listening. If we want to check if someone is breathing, we come as close as we can to that heartbeat and we are very quiet. We lean carefully over that person, almost holding our own breath, so as to be fully in tune with that pulsing whisper.

If we want to absorb with all our being what someone we love is saying or feeling, we sit very quietly, suspend all our verbalizing and enjoy the space that sustains us both. We realize the inadequacy of words and the power of silence whenever we brush closely a moment of love, of deep pain, of reverent tenderness.

In delightful moments of communion with nature, we tread silently and we refrain from speech. The deer will reveal itself only to the self-contained observer. The dove will eat bread from the hand only of the quiet giver. The sound of the brook and the grandeur of forest trees are lost if words trespass. To be somehow in contact with the sap rising in the trees, the tiny sprouts surfacing the soil and the wisps of colour in a twilight sky, we must close our lips and put away all our words. Stand still and enter the mysterious silence of a profound panorama of artistry and harmony and exchange.

In those moments when we yearn to be wrapped in the cloak of God's mercy or are touched by the pulse of God's power, we stretch ourselves past language and we rest in silence. We surrender our arguments and our requests. We discard our carefully worded apologies and our litanies of complaints and we open ourselves to the quiet influence of the Spirit: stirring the waters within, breathing new life into our weary selves, forming for us more trusting and faithful hearts.

In a word, we must practise being alone and silent, with friends, with creation, and with the Spirit who dwells within us. We must trade in our cheap conversations and small talk as unworthy of our time, and as unworthy gifts for those around us. We must learn to listen to the silence of the dawning day, and to speak the secret language of eye and hand and heart. We must allow our experiences to enter our souls and find there some response before we verbalize them and lose their intimate resonance. We must build into our day and our environment times and places of retreat. We must teach our children the value of their own corner and their own private hour. We must convert prayers into prayer, engaging the whole of our being and not only our lips and tongue.

Our world is in dire need of silence. Areas of silent wilderness are being consumed by the greed and schemes of human progress. God is portrayed as hard of hearing and difficult to contact. Hence the noisiness of our liturgies and the wordiness of our supplications. Our places of pilgrimage have been coopted by tourists. People cannot hear one another above the din of their confusion. Who will dare to protect the rare resource of silence and offer it to a world growing deaf from its own loudness?

Learning non-violence

We need to be formed into non-violent communities, providing an antidote to the poisonous violence that eats away at the fabric of our society. We need to become soil that absorbs violence and nurtures gentleness and compassion. Violence is such a condition of our world, we are forced to wonder if it is integral to human nature. I sat at the lake one day puzzled by a swan sitting motionless on a bank near sun-bathers and wading children. Then I realized it had been injured, attacked perhaps by another swan. Just then a boy of seven or eight approached it with a heavy stick and mercilessly struck the cowering bird. He forced the disabled swan to move into the shallow water, back into further danger. It was a cruel and irrational act. And so often violence is. Innocent victims. Sporadic outbursts. Unnecessary brutality.

Do we learn violence from our surroundings? Do we breathe it in with street noises and crowds? What breeds it? Our fear of one another? Or is our fear of one another the result of violence? Who can decipher the mad spiral? Are people who grow up in violent homes or in conflict-ridden countries carriers? Or are they less prone because of their experiences of its toll? Are our handguns and craze for speed and television thrillers its effects? Do we hold life cheaper because there are more of us? Is life more expendable because abortion is legal and wars feed the economy? Where did it all begin and how can we stand in its devastating path? Is it even possible to be non-violent in our world of nuclear weapons and suicidal sports and vicious competition? Is violence justified in liberation struggles, in the struggle for a homeland, in self-defence? And is violence an area where we Christians have been deeply coopted by the societies in which we live?

Our capitulation to the violence around us almost prevents us from recognizing it. In much of the western world our sensitivities have been dulled by our immersion in the rat-race of our careers and the pressures on our personal lives. We are still discriminating enough to reject military violence. Though there are enough households that will relinquish a son to support an army. We also reject the violence of organized injustice: racial discrimination, child pornography, political corruption. But more subtle violence erodes our values and infiltrates our personal priorities. We accept the symbols of success and the stimuli to power, hoping against hope that no violence will result. We silently acquiesce in the violence of a consumer mentality, the violence of apathy and the violence of misinformation from the media. We gulp our food, ignore our human needs for sleep and for play. We insert violence into our language, and we send our children off to play violent games. We try not to notice the violence of our churches in their treatment of women, in the contradictions they embody, in their neglect of some and refusal of others. We squirm at mention of the double-standard in our own lives. And at the scandal of our Christian profession watered down to what is secure and comfortable.

Is it possible that we can lift a non-violent voice, be formed into non-violent witnesses? What will it take? A secure rooting in the gospel of Jesus and the example of those who have taken it seriously: Gandhi, Martin Luther King, Dorothy Day, Desmond Tutu, the women of Greenham Common. The support of a believing community and times of prayerful discernment. A young sister in my own community is gracefully showing the rest of us the way by her commitment to the practice and price of non-violence. Her letters to us from jail after an act of civil disobedience have opened poignant places and aroused our less-tender consciences.

A willingness to be dispossessed, especially of prestigious positions and our latent prejudices. A deep belief in the power of life over death, as actions fail and results are insignificant, even among our close contacts. Eventually and ultimately, a willingness to die rather than kill. A willingness to disarm ourselves in the face of violence. A willingness to suffer the consequences of peace-making to the point of injury and death.

We can test our conversion to non-violence in our own lives. Our response when we are attacked, verbally. Our daily efforts to be trustworthy stewards of creation and ambassadors of reconciliation. Our ability to examine the roots of violence in our own behaviour. The sacrifices we are willing to make to protest the abuse of others and in witnessing for peace.

Recently I saw the film *Testament*, a depiction of the aftermath of nuclear war as it affects a single family. My reaction to the film was curious. I felt no particular fear or urgency to act. I merely wanted to drive home carefully, to note the sinking sun, to invite my community to pray with me. Perhaps our first and repeated resolution must be: to be of all living things more careful, to handle life and its precious moments more gently.

Learning ecumenism

We need to be formed ecumenically, to take more seriously the mandate of Jesus: "There shall be one flock, one shepherd..." and "that all may be one, that the world may believe that you sent me" (John 10:16, 17:21). We must prepare soil in which seeds of unity have a chance to mature and bear fruit. We are at present a scattered, fragmented flock. Our names betray us: Roman Catholics, Greek Orthodox, Anglican Church of Australia, Evangelical Lutheran Church of Finland... We betray our vocation to love one another, to respect and honour our differences, to gather in the name of Jesus Christ as a single sign of his ongoing presence. We betray our identity as the body of Christ. As members of that body, we have obstructed the life that is meant to flow freely. We live without awareness of the gifts and functions of other parts, without a living sense of our common mission. We are disobedient in our persistence in isolating and insulating ourselves from one another. In our stubbornness in clutching our own rituals and doctrines and claiming the wholeness of our partial truths. In our reluctance to learn from and encourage one another in the difficult tasks of justice and peace.

Most of all, we betray the very gift Jesus offered us as his memorial. Before he left them, Jesus gathered his first flock and instructed them to make the breaking of bread and the sharing of wine the mark of their identity and their unity as his disciples. How far we are from honouring that last commission! The most glaring scandal of Christianity is its division over the eucharist, its unwillingness to distribute bread and wine to all who approach the table. What do we think we are doing when we gather around an altar and re-enter that Paschal event? Is it the secret ritual of a private club? Or a banquet of sinners? Is it a matter of theological agreement and doctrinal purity, or is it a question of the law of love transcending our doctrinal limits? Is it some private heritage, some denomination's individually-owned prerogative, the privilege of the elite? Or is it an act performed in the spirit and the name of Jesus? A meal of love and remembrance. A pledge of our commitment to live and die as Jesus did, being broken and poured out for others. Can the life of Jesus be possessed and doled out by certain historically privileged groups? Or is it available now, as in Jerusalem and Galilee, for all who would seek access?

Not only are we Christian churches a conundrum to ourselves, we are a stumbling block to those around us. What impression do we give the uninitiated by our denominational jargon and our doctrinal disputes? What do they conclude when they chance upon our rivalries, our segregation, our hesitancies to minister to those outside our narrow boundaries? And what is their reaction to the shocking realities of Christian warfare, brothers and sisters in the faith engaged in outrageous and contradictory violence, sometimes in the very name of Christ? How can the world believe that this divided and fragmented assemblage is the body of Christ? And when will we realize that our ecumenical pilgrimage as churches is an integral part of our becoming a united community globally?

How can we be formed to counteract this travesty and to build a hope in our eventual unity? During most of my years of education and initial formation, I rarely thought of other Christians, even less of those of other faiths. I did not reject them, or even judge them, I simply never encountered them. Now I realize the deprivation involved. My Christianity remained one-dimensional and my notion of church was more nearly an enclave. The world that did not yet believe somehow vaguely included all those who were not Roman Catholic. The ignorance and consequences of that view are now much clearer to me. As are the historical sins and perpetuated prejudices of my own tradition.

What will arouse in us the spirit of Pentecost? A spirit of bold proclamation and daring deeds? A spirit that will not rest until our hearts are renewed in obedience, our churches hospitable, our tables open? For many like me, even informed instruction has been minimal. In church history we studied the Reformation. Luther and Calvin and Knox were personalities not unlike Chaucer and Dante and Rousseau. I failed to search or to be led into the implications of their lives and visions for my own religious journey. Protestantism and Orthodoxy were matters of history, not matters for ecumenism.

Two years of novitiate, a doctorate in philosophy, and a respectable number of theology courses did not yield a unit or an assignment or an actual experience of ecumenism. I dare say that despite Vatican II a similar lacuna exists in many of our houses of study and seminaries today. My teachers were not opposed, I'm sure, to church unity. It simply wasn't in the curriculum or a need felt by students.

It was only when I entered the realm of social concerns, peace efforts and justice issues, that I found myself in an ecumenical milieu. I did not think of us as Protestants and Roman Catholics as we prepared prayer services and press releases, marched before our federal building and met with Congressional leaders. We were Christians endeavouring to hear and follow the gospel. In the process I visited Protestant churches, participated in their worship, and invited them to mine. A major event in my ecumenical formation was the friendship and the spiritual bond that developed between me and a Methodist pastor, resulting in our common fast for peace.

My ecumenical interest and investment became a central focus when I found a soul-mate in a British Anglican. It is the story of that friendship and that pursuit of a joint mission that has placed the call to unity at the very heart of my life and my ministry. We began a joint prayer-discipline even when we were an ocean apart. We shared our histories and our personal gifts. And we found ourselves invited by the "go-between God" to become an ecumenical team, to live something that would concretize church unity. Since that time of introduction we have literally crossed continents, reflecting in small ways this one sign of the kingdom. The script unfolded for us at Hartford, Connecticut, when we stood in the Cathedral of St Joseph and shared our beliefs with the Presbyterian Church of the US. And the road led to Geneva and Vancouver, where we realized the dream of an ecumenical prayer cell and participation in an assembly of the world church. This book is part of that joint mission.

We have been led inward also, as our bonds have deepened, as a common history has been written, and as we have shared the pains and joys of companionship in the spirit. Our dream continues to evolve, of an ecumenical community committed to enfleshing one particular vision of the gospel in our times. The scenario is so much larger than the two of us, and our response can only be to extend the links and deepen the exchange wherever and however we can. To obey that current of communication initiated somewhere in the realm of the Spirit.

I detail this personal narrative because I believe it is an example precisely of ecumenical formation. In the persons of those who struggle with us for justice, who believe with us in the power of the Holy Spirit, who share a dream of common witness and common worship, we meet the ecumenical movement. We open ourselves to the insights and questions and the spiritual treasures of another part of the body of Christ, and we are deepened and enriched. We pray and work and plan together. We count on each other as resource, as critic, as inspiration, and as friend. We discover ourselves united in the most profound places of our spirits and we yearn to make more visible the truth and the fruits of our unity. We dream on of ecumenical families (often called mixed marriages), of ecumenical programmes of education, of ministry, of ecumenical communities, of further styles of exchange. We empty ourselves of our more arrogant opinions and become more integrated representatives of our own traditions. We cross over into the faith and the practice of Christians and Hindus and Jews, so that the family of God might meet and know still another face of God. We build attitudes and live lives open to the event of a united human community. We do this because we believe that the words of Jesus were spoken of us: "I have given them the glory you gave me that they may be one, as we are one" (John 17:22). Because we believe we are in faith and in the Spirit the body of Christ.

In the process and the plan of our own spiritual formation, we are the dough and we are the kneaders. We are the clay and we are apprentice-potters. We are the soil and also the seed-bearers. There is room among us for the Ignatius-followers and for the devotees of Francis. The Spirit hovers, assisting the transformation of our stony hearts. The gospel of Jesus continues to challenge us to closer discipleship. The "go-between" God crosses over with us into new territories and new depths within our here-and-now existence. What is the fruit of our growth, of our conversion, for our parched and doubting world? The possibility of another tree planted near running water, yielding fruit in due season, and with leaves that never fade.

4. Conflict

The word became light
The word became history
The word became conflict
The word became indomitable spirit
and sowed its seeds upon the mountains
near the river and in the valley.
And those-of-good-will
heard the angels sing.

Julia Esquivel[1]

The people of our mountains and rivers and valleys are crying for a spirituality that addresses the profound crises and myriad struggles of our times. A spirituality that enters the life and death context that occupies so many human beings. That prays with its hands and feet as well as its lips. That meditates on the anguish of starving people and war-torn regions as well as religious truths and sacred mysteries. That embraces human need as well as the hungers of the spirit. That attends to crises here and now even as it gathers and integrates them into their larger, more comprehensive, meaning.

A spirituality for our times

The crisis of a world encircled by nuclear bases and Trident submarines and missile silos. Recently, I spent some days in a quiet, peaceful village in Norfolk, England. An undisturbed pastoral setting, where people do what they did for centuries: till the earth, tend gardens, mend gutters, and thatch cottage roofs. A flash of a kingfisher's flight, the drone of bees, a landscape broken only by haystacks and humble dwellings. All of it marred and jarred by the steady sound of jet engines overhead. Training flights from a nearby RAF and US air base. The presence of dread and destruction even in this remote part of rural England. How does a spirituality for our times address this ominous intervention, this scene of a world punctuated and penetrated by death-like instruments?

The struggle of people for a land of their own and for homes for their children and future generations. The Palestinians, the Lebanese, and all those caught in the history and politics of the

---

[1] *Threatened with Resurrection*, Elgin, IL, Brethren Press, 1982, p.33.

44

Middle East. The struggle of peoples for freedom: from repression, from injustice, and from civil war. The El Salvadorans and the Guatemalans, the Sri Lankans, the Haitians. The struggle of a people to retain their hard-won liberation and to build a society against the pressures of larger and competing powers. The Nicaraguans and Zimbabweans. The ongoing and convoluted struggles in Ireland, in Iran, in Afghanistan. The waste of human life, blotted out by crossfire, denied a chance to flame and burn and lend warmth and light. The greed of landowners, the politics of power and revenge, the distortion of truth, the unconscionable bartering of weapons and influence. Television scenes of an old man in Beirut dodging bullets as he ventures out for his meagre supplies. Of a group of children chasing a ball amid the rubble of homes and shops. Faces of refugees seeking sanctuary, fleeing from death and horror, in Eastern Africa and Central America. Faces of my own sisters seeking exile in Mexico, fleeing possible kidnapping and death threats in Guatemala. Worshippers murdered in Belfast, famine and torture in Matabeleland, political and religious clashes in the Punjab, despair and powerlessness in the Philippines. Around our world, the suffering of millions, the struggles of centuries, the haunting spectre of death and darkness, the daily realities of hunger and disease and fear. How does a spirituality for our times insert itself into this morass of human misery and offer hope and solace and redemption?

Blatant terrorism in our berserk and disordered world. Guns fired from embassy windows. Political kidnappings and torture. Covered-up murders and death squads. Failing efforts to combat crime, to protect women and the elderly, to ensure safe streets, to defend life in its most vulnerable forms. Domestic crises, resulting in violence and abuse. Youth ensnared in a drug culture. Cities overtaken by deafening noise, gaudy lights, demoralizing advertising, unsightly slums, and unhealthy lifestyles. People forced onto welfare, into soup-kitchen lines, into idleness and lives of despair. A consumer society frenzied in its pursuit of fads, polluted by its preservatives and insecticides, oblivious of its suicidal course. A world of contradictions and catastrophes, flaunting its tawdry wares, marching frantically to its tinny and raucous music, fixed on success and wealth and sophisticated snobbery. A world that snuffs out and ridicules the spiritual, denies the transcendent, and buries itself in artificial dressings and superficial communication. How does a spirituality for our times find a foothold in this decaying and decadent atmosphere?

Of what relevance to campesinos in Latin America, to slum-dwellers in Bombay, to poor blacks in Detroit, to drug-addicts and battered children in San Francisco, is the gospel message of freedom and love? Of what comfort to the evicted family and the unemployed father of five is the story of Lazarus and the rich man? Your reward is forthcoming and your oppressors will suffer. But who of us considers ourselves in the position of the tormented man in hell beseeching Abraham for a drop of water? How do we translate Jesus' narrative into a contemporary warning about the use of our time and resources and our priorities?

How does the Isaiah of today share the word of the Lord regarding fasting? And who is his audience? Is it not perhaps to pious church-goers and Lenten observers, people like ourselves, that the word is addressed? Release those bound unjustly: our Latin neighbours bound by fear of US military aid, illegal aliens bound by their fear of discovery and deportation. Set free the oppressed: the exploited banana-growers in Honduras and the underpaid cotton-growers in Louisiana. Share your bread with the hungry: ferret out the connections between India's poverty and the tremendous waste in the US, between famine in the Horn of Africa and Europe's overstocked granaries. Shelter the oppressed and the homeless: allow that halfway house to locate on your street, and reassess your attitudes to the plight of the Native Americans. The Lord will renew your strength, to take issue with the glib reports of our mass media, and the simplistic solutions of our political parties.

Who among us has the courage to ask in our assemblies and our meeting rooms the hard question: when the Son of Man comes, will he find any faith on the earth (Luke 18:8)? For are not the implications meant for us, who plan programmes to address poverty and injustice, and regularly claim our high salaries and pursue our comfortable life-styles? For us, who preach sacrifice and generosity to our parishioners, and sport our latest-model Oldsmobiles and expensive golf clubs? For us, who profess solidarity with the poor, and continue to build retirement homes and travel in style and dress like our secular counterparts? For us, who read the scriptures, celebrate the eucharist, and call ourselves Christian, while we shun the Samaritans of our day, live in discord, compete for positions, and shirk confrontations with those who perpetrate injustice? The word of the Lord to us is a call to repentance, to open our lives to conversion, and to allow the scriptures to judge and rebuke us.

What does it mean for the harrassed mother who finds herself pregnant to "choose life"? For the prostitute trapped in her web of self-hatred and survival-techniques? For the Polish worker who fears reprisals for his political protest? For the Parisian socialite addicted to her own image and fearful of the signs of ageing? For the company manager, alienated from his own family, forced to compete, dragging himself up the ladder of achievement? For the female theology student on the threshold of ordination, blocked by a church that refuses to recognize women ministers? For the retired farmer whose ample acreage has been replaced by a sunless room in a crowded tenement? "I have today set before you life and prosperity, death and doom" (Deut. 30:15). Who will counsel them? Who will understand their dilemma? Who will offer spiritual discernment as they choose their muddled and compromising way?

The path of discipleship

Of what help then is the gospel in our confusing and conflicting times? And in what possible sense does it contain good news? For whom? For many in our times it requires an invincible faith and an enduring hope to bridge the gap between their private misfortunes and the kingdom promised to them. The gospel has meaning only to those whose lives are open to the Spirit and the total message of Jesus. Who believe that Jesus is now and forever the life of the world, and that his life can be mediated in this time and in this death-filled environment. Who believe that following the gospel injects into the world about us a new stream of life and hope. Who believe that a company of gospel-followers can redeem and renew what is sinful and dying. Who in that belief are willing to stake their lives and declare themselves fools for the sake of Christ. Who dare to be different, to live upside-down lives, to be signs of life, sparks of light, in the midst of death's darkness.

For the one who chooses discipleship such a path means conflict. The one who obeys the gospel mandates will live in tension. The one who makes Jesus' values her own will enter into conflict with the standards of her surroundings. And she will be tested. And tempted to compromise, to surrender, to escape. She will be served the same dilemmas and questions Jesus faced. She will be asked to lay down her life, bit by bit, day by day. In the end her victory will not be sung or celebrated. Her victory will be, like Jesus' own, the seed of her own new life and the seed of life for those with whom she lives and dies. "No slave is greater than his master; no messenger outranks the one who sent him" (John 13:16). To portray the disciple's destiny in any other way is to betray the very meaning of Jesus' life and death. A spirituality that evades this ultimate struggle and commitment is not a spirituality at all. It denies the very premise of our faith: the light shines on in darkness, a darkness that did not overcome it.

In the face of life's serious conflicts, the gospel shapes the disciple. It calls us first of all to lay a firm foundation. "Anyone who hears my words and puts them into practice is like the wise person who built a house on rock" (Matt. 7:24). At the heart of our discipleship is a willingness to live the gospel, to transfer its meaning and its demands into the concrete situations of our current existence. Our best preparation for meeting and overcoming darkness, the darkness of our times, is a habit of living in deed and in truth the words and works of Jesus. "When the rainy season set in, the torrents came and the winds blew and buffeted the house. It did not collapse; it had been solidly set on rock" (Matt. 7:25). By contrast, the person who knows the gospel, even utters it, but does not incarnate it, will fall short in the time of trial. Under the pressure and pain of the cross, that person will collapse (like the house built on sand) and take flight.

Secondly, the gospel places before us the standards of the kingdom and of those who would help build it. We are to be *salt* restoring flavour where life has lost its taste and adding joy. We are to be *light*, witnessing boldly to the priorities of Jesus. We are to be *reconcilers*, approaching God in prayer and worship when we have approached one another with sincere and understanding hearts. We are to be *single-minded*, quick to let go of anything that interferes with our faithfulness to the gospel. We are to be *truth-makers*, avoiding the fuzzy thinking and rationalizing of those who would save their comfortable lives as well as their souls. We are to be *non-violent*, reaching out to our opponents through the heart rather than reason, and disarming them by the force of our love and truth. We are to be *persons of the Spirit*, seeking wisdom in solitude and prayer. We are to be *seekers* first, last, and always, of the kingdom of God, the kingdom of justice and peace and unity, while we trust in the provision of all that is necessary to continue that quest.

Finally, the gospel directs us to the peak of discipleship, to the final witnessing of our faith and our obedience. "This is my commandment: love one another as I have loved you. There is no greater love than this: to lay down one's life for one's friends" (John 15:12-13). A spirituality of conflict leads us necessarily to solidarity with those who suffer and struggle and die. The gospel stretches us to join in spirit, and perhaps in the flesh, the wounded and disfigured body of Christ. To enter into the conflict of our brothers and sisters, their liberation efforts, their cries for justice, their agony and death.

Those who build their spiritual foundation on a rock will experience inner conflict. Easier to discuss the beatitudes than to practise them. Easier to read the Passion, than to recognize it reoccurring in the lives of peasants and political prisoners. Easier to preach the gospel of simplicity and compassion and non-violence than to repent and convert. Those who opt to put the gospel into practice will have to forego the security of their savings. They will have to risk the alienation and misunderstanding of their friends. They will have to pay the price of their association with outcasts and the marginalized.

The conflict within and without will heighten for those who endorse with their lives the values and the ideals of the kingdom. A friend of mine speaks of her commitment to the Catholic Worker House as a constant challenge. Sometimes she dreads opening the door and encountering another mother unable to feed her children, another family lost in the cracks of a welfare system, another mentally disturbed adult rejected by family and neighbours. Some days she resents handing out bags of beans and loaves of bread to persons who have drifted all their lives or who, by their abuse of alcohol and drugs, deprive the more worthy.

In India I watched with awe the indefatigable patience of my companions. Bestowing blankets on the homeless, who then bartered them for food and drink and returned cold and ragged. Dispensing medicines to mothers for children whose bodies were covered with flies and maggots. Entreating in vain a family to leave a patient in the hospital rather than risk dehydration at home. Gathering village children for classes with the sole equipment of slates and pieces of chalk-rock.

My missionary friend in Guatemala lives in a wooden hut and struggles to learn the Indian language. Our letters must be sifted to avoid any discussion of the reality of her situation. She submits every six months to a humiliating blood test for venereal disease in order to secure an extension of her visa. Regularly she travels thirteen hours by mule and bus to maintain contact with her larger Franciscan community.

Last December three of my friends were among those arrested in Michigan for calling attention to the plant making engines for cruise missiles. They were found guilty of littering and trespassing and handed thirty-day sentences. Their ministry continued in jail, in their dialogue with the guards and with us outside.

From such as these and from all those who toil in the Lord's vineyard, we learn lessons of spirituality. Their books are written in sweat and blood. An African leader, frequently threatened, himself imprisoned at times, declares: If God is for us, who can be against? A young woman from the Marshall Islands tells her story of betrayed islanders and misshapen "jellyfish" babies against the backdrop of her own radiation-induced tumors. A Korean pastor describes his Easter morning arrest. A Lebanese man fingers his beads and endures his private agony after news of bombings in the area where his family still resides. Native Americans of Canada hold a silent symbolic vigil on the campus where church officials meet and exchange ecumenical agendas. "Who will separate us from the love of Christ? Trial or distress or persecution or hunger or nakedness or danger or the sword?... I am certain that neither death nor life, neither angels nor principalities, neither the present nor the future, nor powers, neither height nor depth nor any other creature, will be able to separate us from the love of God that comes to us in Christ Jesus, our Lord" (Rom. 8:35-39). Such is the conviction, in the eye of the hurricane, of those obedient to the gospel of Jesus.

Some of Jesus' disciples are asked to enter fully into his passion and death. There is to be no limit to the love and solidarity they extend. Their lives and deaths are gifts to the rest of us as we struggle to realize the full meaning of spiritual discipleship. Our minds are baffled by the seeming loss and our hearts are broken by the depths of their courage and sacrifice. Blessed are we when our lives are touched in a human way by the event of martyrdom. Wayward are we if the effects of such sacrifice are lost and forgotten.

Many of us were pierced by the spiritual commitment of the four American women who were murdered in El Salvador in 1980. For North American women like myself they were our peers and reminded us of people we knew personally in similar circumstances. By crossing the line of risk and identifying with the oppressed, they confronted the evils of economic injustice. Their light shone in the darkness and the darkness attempted to extinguish it. They accompanied the poor of that country on their *via crucis*. No greater love than this. But their light was not extinguished. Those four women live, in the minds and hearts of those of us who take one step further in our identification with the broken and brutalized body of Jesus. They have broken through for all of us into the possibility of that ultimate commitment.

Preparation for conflict

How do we prepare ourselves to enter conflict? Our true human stature is measured by our response to crisis. Spiritually too, our capacity for a faithful response is revealed when we are put to the test. In some ways, daily living with its multiple demands and stresses prepares us for the times of battle. But there are particular experiences that ready our spirits for the day of conflict.

Radicalizing experiences, that is, moments of risk, plunge us into deeper waters than we currently know. All of us accept the importance of such moments in the life of every human being. Bearing a child, undergoing surgery, losing a loved one, necessary separations, marriage itself, require risk and upset our usual and routine patterns. Those involved in the formation of youth try to provide radicalizing experiences (sometimes called initiation rites). For some of us a bus-trip into our inner cities alters our perspective. Or a conversation with a Buddhist or a Muslim. A woman who had never known poverty or discrimination was shocked into action when her son was jailed for theft. A college student changed his academic direction and became a community organizer after a summer in the slums of Mexico City. For me, the day of my arrival in Bombay provided as much radicalization as I could then bear. My first encounter with stark poverty and overwhelming misery. I had quickly to come to terms with my western identity and my personal inner resources. Unforgettable markings on my spirit, unseasoned and over-protected.

Such are the effects of entering radically different realms, realms that open our eyes, jar our habitual mindsets and values and force us to re-evaluate our attitudes and our actions. They put into the balance what is familiar and acceptable to us and challenge us to go deeper, to enlarge our narrow ideas and our reluctant hearts. We break with our clean, orderly, intellectual arguments and enter unthought-of and undescribed realities. We are never again quite the same. We lose some of our complacency and we are humbled by our inability to adapt and our limited understanding of life. We are also forever opened to further risk and further adventure. Radicalizing experiences are baptisms of the spirit, preparation for living in new ways, closer to the fragile humanity we share with our remotest neighbours.

Times of prayer and reflection, of serious examination of our truth and our commitment, are also important dimensions of our spiritual preparation. Self-knowledge, so difficult to come by, so elusive and so easily confused with whispers of pride and of ego, enables us to gain perspective and to assess our motives. We have abundant examples of the soul-searching that precedes entrance into battle: the words of Thomas More and Charles de Foucauld, the poetry of Julia Esquivel and Mari Angelou, the homilies of Oscar Romero and Martin Luther King. The deeper and the more serious the journey within, the more credible and sustainable our journey into exterior danger. Only those who possess their own souls, know their own weaknesses and strengths, are ready to embrace the hardships and the harsh realities of surrounding struggles. Only those who are in touch with their own inner streams of grace and truth have something to offer their companions in conflict. Inner freedom is a prerequisite for solidarity with those who are oppressed and in agony. It is in disciplined prayer and the rigours of solitude and discernment that we discover our true resources and the most appropriate response to an ensuing combat.

Many of us in Milwaukee were affected in the early 1970s by the spirituality of a committed layman. Married, with six children, Michael Cullen was involved in the most radical of activities: counselling draft resisters, civil disobedience, and directing a house of hospitality for transients and outcasts. But he also prayed the psalms, baked coarse brown bread, taught his children hymns, and reflected with groups on the meaning of non-violence. Clearly, his roots in prayer and meditation sustained him during his jail sentence and eventual deportation. He was ready to undergo the consequences of his choices and he did so with inner calm and freedom. His behaviour, on a daily basis and under duress, moved us deeply and influenced our own sense of obedience to the gospel. We saw in Michael a concrete and credible witness to non-violence and to the transforming power of prayer.

I believe it is difficult to enter arenas of conflict and to choose to suffer with the oppressed without the support and encouragement of a faith-community. In a general way that is precisely the meaning of our baptism into a specific Christian community. We are surrounded by the company of those who believe and who inspire us to act and to risk. In an atmosphere of acceptance and common vision, we are enabled to interpret the meaning of the gospel and to place our lives in relationship to it. In a time of personal crisis, the community becomes for us a strength, a refuge, a place of healing and restoration. And in a time of entanglement with the powers of darkness and evil, we rely upon its combined resources. It is within the context of community that we call upon the guidance of the Spirit and search the direction in which we are being led. Those standing with us or behind us loan us their strength and their hope. We benefit from the way we are held in their prayer and their concern. We bring more to the task than our individual power and insights.

We carry with us the ardour and energy stemming from those bonds.

How else do we explain the endurance and spirit of the women of Greenham Common? Or the fearlessness and determination of those who make a peace witness in Nicaragua? Or the vitality and resilience of a group like Sojourners? Only through the strength of a community could my friends in India bear the daily burdens and engender so much light and hope in the midst of so much despair. It is the power of a community that sustains those at St Benedict's who minister to the poorest of Milwaukee's poor. A real community, gathered in Jesus' name, is compelled to take its gospel to the streets and to the halls of the mighty and to the nuclear unfree zones. The burden is less wearying and the threats less ominous when we walk in the company of other pilgrims and other seekers of the kingdom. Sharing our faith renews it. The steadfastness of others re-enkindles our flagging hope. And the clasped hands and embracing eyes of our companions impel us to greater acts of love. The journey into difficult situations becomes not only plausible, but the very site of our growth in spirituality and exchange.

Our divided and discordant world reveals to us the larger side of our own divided and discordant hearts. A spirituality of conflict cannot ignore the tensions that exist in each of us, the brokenness and fragmentation. It will be difficult to accompany others on missions of reconciliation and liberation if we neglect the inner tasks of healing and emancipating. Some of us are imprisoned in our fears and prejudices. Most of us are captives of our society's values and our culture's blindnesses. We must undertake a journey into freedom if we would attempt to defend and guarantee the freedom and dignity of others. Some of us are wounded by past events and childhood deprivations. Scarred by betrayals and the discouragement of our own failures. Stunted by the narrowness of our own visions and crippled by the demands of our egos and our unbridled desires. We must seek wholeness and an acceptance of ourselves and our history if we would be messengers of healing and integrity to our neighbours.

Some of us are paralyzed by our life-styles and our success-seeking, loaded down with possessions and investments, cluttered up with titles and degrees and appointment books, so that we can't possibly set foot on a pilgrim path. Letting go, of unessentials and encumbrances and superfluous baggage, is a spiritual task that precedes peace-making missions and an option for the poor. Perhaps most of us western Christians are caught in the ambivalence of our middle-class identities, our multiple responsibilities, and the uncertainties of a life of risk. We confess our hesitancy to reform our lives and our reluctance to be gospel-people. We recognize our most flagrant idolatries, and take small steps to curtail our addictions. But we are not yet ready to hear the unambiguous call of the gospel and to stand in its transparent light. We remain on the sidelines, clinging to our double option, to enter the fray or to evade the summons a bit longer.

Anointing our youth

Our tradition has long acknowledged and even exalted spiritual warfare. Anointing with oil is a sacred act because it signifies the graces of fortitude and perseverance needed in battle. At our confirmation each of us was consecrated for a life of conflict. We accepted our vocation as holy warriors. In some of our ceremonies today we anoint those chosen to be leaders among us, or those sent on distant and difficult missions. We are reminded that we draw our strength from God. "Our battle is not against human forces but against the principalities and powers... Stand fast, with truth as the belt around your waist, justice as your breastplate, and zeal to propagate the gospel of peace as your footgear... hold faith up before you as your shield... take the helmet of salvation and the sword of the spirit, the word of God" (Eph. 6:12-17).

In that spirit the early Christian martyrs withstood the taunts and derisions of their persecutors. They renounced idolatry and refused to compromise. There have been many distortions, however, of the notion of spiritual battle. The Crusaders launched religious wars and the reformers and counter-reformers excommunicated and eradicated one another in a zeal for doctrine and presumptuous claims to the truth. Persons like St Francis of Assisi turned the military approach upside down and, while retaining zeal and a thirst for justice, lay down their arms and fought with the weapons of simple truth and human compassion. Francis sought to confront the evils of his day with the scandalous testimony of his voluntary poverty and his respect and reverence for all of creation. His response to hatred and injury was to sow seeds of love and pardon. Francis was not naive about the powers and forces of darkness, but neither would he battle with them on their own terms. Legend says he tamed a dangerous wolf with a gesture of acceptance and trust. He entered the presence of the Sultan of Egypt without the protection of arms. He surrendered the reins of government of his own organization to disloyal innovators. He identified so closely with the Passion of his Lord that his flesh was branded with similar wounds. Many have been faithful to his style of non-violence and his association with the poor and down-trodden. Such is the saga of the martyrs of Latin America today, and the witness of Dom Helder Camara, Dorothy Day, Lanzo del Vasto, Cesar Chavez and Jean Vanier.

Perhaps it is exactly this style of enduring and waging conflict that could engage our contemporary youth. Our secular society offers enough models of militant aggression and enough experiences of training camps and military rites. We might counter such experiences with a pilgrimage of peace-making and of intercultural and ecumenical sharing. We might anoint our youth for the specific twentieth century task of studying history, understanding cultures, and bridging the gaps between north and south, east and west. We might lead them on international pilgrimages, allowing them to imbibe the spirit of bygone fervent eras and the heritage of Mother Julian and Francis of Assisi and Martin Luther and Mohandas Gandhi. We might train them in methods of prayer and the hymns of the ages and embark them on a spiritual adventure that includes cathedrals and hermitages, nuclear sites and vivisection laboratories. We might send them on foot, to tramp the ground others walked, to visit the villages hallowed by time and suffering, to climb the mountains of inspiration and retreat. We might equip them with the symbols of solidarity: bread, the scriptures, and open hands. We might encourage them to abide awhile in peace camps and refugee centres and to join harvesting crews and urban renewal teams.

The warfare waged might be that of spirituality versus selfishness, freedom versus fear, and understanding and appreciation versus ignorance and condescension. We might form a new kind of army, a pilgrim-army, honouring creation, forging connections, and creating harmony among the human family. We might all find new sanity as we walk and ponder together, and a new spirituality for our times as well. What a different purpose served from the presence of our US youth in Beirut and Grenada and behind protected military fences around the world! What a different journey and a different dream for our misguided urban adolescents who cruise our highways in revved-up motors and idle their time in game rooms and shopping malls. What a different antidote for the ennui and apathy of a generation groping for spiritual models and meaningful ideals.

The hope that is in us

It was Teilhard de Chardin who taught us that hope always has the final word. We look around our war-riddled and gravely disfigured world and we see shining beacons of hope. In our midst there are persons and groups whose lives testify to the spirituality of combat they have embraced. Whether our context be that of South African apartheid or the militarized Philippines, the Latin American struggle for liberation or resistance to US military aggression, we find those who declare boldly their commitment to justice and peace. Putting their lives at risk. Enduring the deprivations of prison. Voicing the convictions of their faith. Sustaining the weaker among us in our resolve to struggle and to overcome. They are seeds of a new community, sparks of life in a world darkened by sinful indifference and blatant malice.

Anglican Bishop Desmond Tutu is hope in action in his continued confrontations with the South African government on behalf of the oppressed and the uprooted poor. Lay church worker Karl Gaspar is a prayer of hope as he continues his human rights ministry from his prison cell in Davao City. Larry Rosebaugh, Catholic priest, echoes the risks of his African and Philippine brothers. For years he identified with the poor of America's inner cities, in Milwaukee and in Recife. Now he resists US military might and its destructive tentacles that reach even into barrios and refugee camps. He testifies to his hope from a federal prison in Texas.

I confess that on my own journey there have been minimal risks and limited commitments to struggle in solidarity. Fear has not been foreign to me, even physical fear, because of circumstances in which I was vulnerable or because of feelings of alienation. I experienced some such moments in India when I felt victimized by the indifference and scorn of people, themselves victims of western imperialism and exploitation. There are only a few instances in my life in which I felt actual threat from the forces around me, forces of darkness and injustice. One such experience occurred within the last year, in my own country and while within the walls of a Catholic church.

Our church of St Benedict's was among those supporting sanctuary for Latin American refugees. I found myself involved in the actual implementation. Luis came to us from El Salvador via California. He was a family man, a factory worker, himself committed to the political impact of the sanctuary movement. I became one of those who formed a community for Luis. For the first weeks we kept an around-the-clock presence in the church, as interpreter, as companion and friend. Each time I arrived for my shifts, I felt some fear. Why was that car following me? Who might be lurking on the church parking lot? What were those knocking sounds we heard from Luis's sacristy room? We all knew we were subject to a fine and/or prison if arrested. We had the phone number of a volunteer lawyer at hand. We also rehearsed with Luis the responses we must give if and when a search warrant was issued. Daily I smuggled Luis in and out of the church to the rectory near by, for a shower and a change of scenery. My fear of arrest was doubled by the realization that my involvement could jeopardize a pending ecumenical venture in Europe. In my more honest moments, I also knew I was afraid of jail, of the physical inflictions and the psychic strain. My fears were relieved when Luis was able to move out of the church, without incident and without arrest or deportation. What I remember now are the Spanish phrases Luis taught me, the tortillas we shared, and the joy I felt when Luis could discard the protective mask he wore in public and become an ordinary member of our Sunday congregation.

What is the reason for the hope that is in you? A question we might well ask Luis. Or those who refuse to accept the indignities and injustices of apartheid. Or the political prisoners who sit in solitary confinement, refusing to cooperate with the prison system, having many times over refused to cooperate with the military establishment. Or those who serve soup and distribute clothing and offer hospitality to those stripped of all but the last vestige of life. "My grace is sufficient for you, for in weakness power reaches perfection. Therefore I am content with weakness, with mistreatment, with distress, with persecutions and difficulties for the sake of Christ; for when I am powerless, it is then that I am strong" (2 Cor. 12:9-10).

We do not doubt that their hope and their identification with Christ exist. We see the triumph of the human spirit in the midst of pain and hellish deprivation. We see the transforming effects on others of suffering borne willingly, with dignity, in the cause of justice. We see the liberated spirits of those who know to whom they belong, who have placed their bodies on the line, who live in and for the kingdom. We are awed by the friendship they extend, the songs they sing, the quality of their celebrations. In their presence we sense that "cloud of witnesses" that has gone before and that leads us now into the Galilees and the Gethsemanes of our world. We believe that life emerges out of their death, that their mourning will be turned into dancing (Ps. 30:12-13) and that they who sow in tears will reap rejoicing (Ps. 126:5-6).

Once again we ponder the meaning of those paradoxes: the light shines on in darkness, we are strong when we are weak, the word became conflict. On my part I acknowledge that I have not reaped the fruits of a spirituality of conflict. For I grapple still with the mystery of those pronouncements. I need to stand longer in the sandals of a pilgrim. I need to enter more often into the camps of the exiled and the ranks of the down-trodden. I need to ponder more carefully the lessons of history and the living memories of those who died in the struggle for freedom. I need to bend closer to the heart of Francis and listen more intently to his testimony. I need to take more seriously the gospel call to sell all and leave all. The most difficult of the gospel words have not penetrated my conscience and my behaviour. My life has not yet been inverted by the beatitudes or split open by the contradictions of peace and the sword, of laying down one's life and yielding lasting fruit. I am reluctant to become identified with the naked, thorn-crowned, spat-upon, crucified Christ. "Lord, I am not yet willing for you to have your way with me, but I am willing to be made willing."[2]

---

[2] An ancient prayer attributed to St Teresa of Avila.

5. Obedience

*One day when Jesus was praying in seclusion and his disciples
were with him, he put the question to them: "Who do the crowds
say that I am?" "John the Baptist," they replied, "and some say
Elijah, while others claim that one of the prophets of old has
returned from the dead." "But you – who do you say that I
am?" he asked them (Luke 9:18-20a).*

Perhaps the disciples were caught off guard. It is one thing to
be asked what the crowds make of Jesus. It is entirely a different
matter to confess one's own thoughts and perceptions. Who do
you say that I am?

A personal question

What are your images of God, of Jesus Christ, of the Spirit?
Perhaps the crowds say God is absent or dead, or that God is
intervener and judge. Perhaps the crowds say that Jesus is a
fanatic, a sentimentalist, a one-time prophet and trouble-maker.
Or that the Spirit of God is too ephemeral and too abstract for
any meaningful discussion. And the crowds prefer to be obedient to the laws of nature and the wisdom of their own plans.
They opt to follow the signals of financial experts, scientific
futurists, and practitioners of business and industry. But who do
you say that I am? We already hear echoes: suffering, rejection,
death, and resurrection on the third day. And we hear another
echo: I was hungry and you gave me food. A stranger and you
welcomed me. In prison and you visited me. As often as you did
it for one of my sisters or brothers... (Matt. 25:35-40). Images
of judgment, of radical behaviour, of a united kingdom.

We strive to listen to the soft breeze and the still, small voice.
To listen long and often. To the word of God when and where it
is spoken. Allowing God to say what we may not want to hear.
Listening with our heart, so that we are prepared to recognize
God in our world, in creation, in our times, in people. And we
learn to wait for our own deafness to be healed, for life to be less
absurd and more transparent. We wait for the message: "I have
waited, waited for the Lord, and he stooped towards me and
heard my cry" (Ps. 40:2). We wait silently, in anticipation, in
confidence. And acknowledge that we do fail to meet God, even
when God's name is written all over our agendas, even when
God gives us the miracle we say we need in order to believe.

Images of obedience from a context of spirituality. Not the context of theological reasoning or of psychology's super-ego. Not the claims of power or superiority or driving desperation. Not the casualties of a false, blind obedience, that denies responsibility and deserts integrity. The obedience of the gospel, of Jesus to his Father, of the disciple to the master. The obedience that is summed up in the Philippians: "Though he was in the form of God, he did not deem equality with God something to be grasped at. Rather, he emptied himself and took the form of a slave, being born in human likeness. He was known to be of human estate, and it was thus that he humbled himself, obediently accepting even death, death on a cross" (2:6-8).

Letting go

How do we find our way into that style and spirit of obedience? What images will we have to absorb and enflesh as we set our feet upon the path of Jesus, a path marked by self-emptying, solidarity with the human condition, and humble acceptance of the agony of the cross? Often in the gospels we are pointed towards the experience of "letting go" and "letting in". Our lives are often so cluttered and clogged with noise and motion and trivia that neither God's word nor God's grace can enter. Let go of your fishing nets, your hardened opinions and stereotypes, your fear of human judgment, your grudges, your lifeless traditions. Let in the Spirit's promptings, the message of today's prophets, the songs and hymns of creation, the cries of the lonely and the abandoned, the new wine of enthusiasm and zeal. Learn to say good-bye, to allow your plans to be changed, to accept the ageing process.

Practising a new asceticism prepares us for obedient response. For some of us that means the asceticism of meetings, of steady dialogue and discussion. Tempered by the truth of those encounters and the monitoring of their results. Or the asceticism of devotion to children, denying ourselves the convenience and luxury of private space and time. We find our asceticism today in fasting, not only from food, but from all things harmful to bodies and spirits. In maintaining sincere lines of communication, refusing entrance to polite untruths and manipulative compliments. Our spiritual exercises include the use of sun and fresh air, the stewardship of our gifts and talents, the budgeting of our time, and the honest assessment of our relationships. Rather than discipline our bodies, we western Christians need to free them from the dangers of obesity, the perils of polluted air and water, the restrictions of fashionable dress and the captivity of desk and office. Rather than tame our spirits we need to unleash our creative impulses, give wings to our imaginations, and experiment with all manner and styles of prayer. Rather than bend and bridle our wills, we need to channel their energies into works of value, into feats of faith and of bold pioneering.

A renewed asceticism enables us to empty ourselves of false claims to heroism and sanctity. It puts us in touch with the fragile reality and the frail beauty of our human nature. Similarly, a discipline of prayer empties us of our petty preoccupations and opens us to the celebration of our creaturehood and the diverse pleas of the human community. Our personal prayer and meditation merge with times of common search and moments of holy communion. We learn to pray with many voices: the weeping sounds of those who mourn, the insistent cries of those who struggle, the agonizing whispers of those overwhelmed by life, the confident voices of children, the musical raptures of those in love, the babbling bursts of those fully alive and fully grateful. The world in all its grandeur and all its fragmentation enters our prayer, and our prayer inspirits our world of encounters and anxieties and shortcomings. In prayer we learn to let go of our own designs, to follow the uncharted course of freedom and obedience. We let go of our role-playing and our deceitful masks, to become simply and starkly beginners on the road to truth and wholeness. Prayer reminds us that we are not self-sufficient and indispensable. It surprises us with glimpses of purity and wisdom. Prayer clears our vision and renews our appetite for mystery and mysticism. Prayer softens our clotted hearts and stirs our abandoned dreams, while it finds utterance for our sorrow and our shame. Prayer quickens us to receive the angel of the Lord in whatever disguise. And beckons us into territories yet unknown and tasks yet untried. In our prayer we stand in the solid company of the saints as we embrace the length and breadth and depth of the human family. Our prayer exposes the degree of our willingness to undergo a kenosis with Christ.

Loving entails letting go. People do not belong to us, we learn through many experiences of surrender and of loss. They become an intimate part of us when we let go of them in love. Everyone we let go of, we find on a deeper level. Having lost the security of possessing others, we are free to be present to them, to exchange life with them, and to experience the response of their trust. "He who bends to himself a Joy/Doth the winged life destroy;/But he who kisses the Joy as it flies,/Lives in Eternity's sunrise."[1]

Perhaps there is no more human journey into kenosis than that of the self-emptying that love prompts. Gradually, but surely, love leads us to abandon some of our private dreams and ambitions. Leads us to adapt our schedules and our styles of receiving and sharing. Love demands that we unveil ourselves and inhabit each other's inner worlds. In the ecstasy of our exchange we immerse ourselves freely and offer ourselves fully to the other. Love of another human being is as close as we can come to understanding the marvel and the mystery of Jesus' incarnation. In love we bear the burdens and share the joys of the beloved. We stand outside ourselves, as much as it is humanly possible, and live in tune with the other's heart and spirit. "Do not try to direct the course of love, for love, if it finds you worthy, will direct you."[2]

A supple heart

The ability to let go, to abandon oneself in faith and obedience, creates a heart that is docile and humble. Both notions are fairly foreign to our independent, stubborn, self-reliant, spirits. Both virtues are fairly absent in our assertive, self-confident, self-indulgent, circles. But uncovering their meaning and their message to us twentieth century Christians is crucial for a spirituality of our times. Dag Hammarskjöld described a moment of docility that reverberated throughout his entire life: "I don't know who or what put the question. I don't know when it was put. I don't even remember answering. But at some moment I did answer Yes to Someone, or Something, and from

---

[1] William Blake, *Selected Poems*, London, Oxford University Press, 1951, p.121.
[2] Kahlil Gibran, *The Prophet*, London, Heinemann, 1969, p.12.

that hour I was certain that existence is meaningful and that, therefore, my life, in self-surrender, had a goal."[3]

Docility is the Yes to the challenges and invitations life offers us. Docility belongs to the heart kept supple by frequent and regular exercise. The exercise of submitting to a higher wisdom and a deeper word. Of adapting our private and personal priorities to match more closely the bidding of the gospel. Of turning ourselves around when we would stand still and of picking up a burden just when we would lay it aside. Docility is the ability to respond affirmatively when voices within us insist we say No. Don't look back when your hand is at the plough. Don't return home to bury the dead. Don't tell anyone the vision. Don't fear those who hurt the body, but cannot destroy the soul. Don't exalt yourself or vie for positions of glory. Do cast your nets for a catch. Do return to give thanks. Do go out like sheep among wolves. Do become like little children. Do forgive seventy times seven times.

Most of us learn docility, if we learn it, the long, hard way of trial and ordeal. We learn it in small events as preparation for a more total surrender. We become seasoned by our repeated mistakes, experiences of illness and rejection, and the unfolding of a hidden design in the fragments of our lives. Our waiting ends in surprised joy, our time of testing results in a stronger faith, our fear of failure converted into the healing balm of the truth. For too long, and for some good reasons, we have associated docility with a naive submission and the weakness of a compliant character. As with non-violence, we have viewed docility as passive. And we have interpreted strength as a resistance to anything that diminishes our individual power and prerogatives.

Only when our images shift and enlarge will we appreciate the spiritual value of a docile and humble heart. In the season of Pentecost we pray: make supple what is stiff. It is the inflexible and rigid heart that cannot avail itself of the breath and the wind of the Spirit. It stands unyielding and unbending, constrained in its lack of spontaneity. We also pray: make straight what is false and warped. Most often we contrast humility with pride. And it is a valid opposition. But if we remember that humility is the

[3] *Markings*, New York, Alfred A. Knopf, 1965, p.205.

truth of one's condition, then it is rightly opposed to falsity, to a warped version of reality. Rather than detract from our status, docility and humility add to it. The ability to be flexible and to integrate the unexpected, and the uprightness to acknowledge the truth of our being. The humble in our midst are not those who go around, eyes downcast, effacing themselves and their achievements, and allowing themselves to be stepped on or passed over. Rather, they are those whose eyes reveal their inner truth, whose lives and deeds are clear enough for all to assess, and who stand on the sure ground of honesty and sincerity. The test of greatness in a person is an ability to recognize the littlest and lowliest, to be available to ordinary people, and to remember his or her own simple roots. The humble are those without pretence and vanity, liberated from the need for publicity and constant recognition. Your very words will testify on your behalf. Seek the glory that comes from God. The truth will set you free. If you love your life, you will lose it. Apart from the source of your life and gifts, you are nothing. Wash one another's feet.

Only when we accept our own broken condition and believe in the gratuitous love of God can we afford to live and act with humility. Only when we are not consumed by a competitive spirit, or ensnared by our delusions of importance, or desperate for the outer accoutrements of success. We enter the dwelling places of humility when we experience grace in tents as well as in cathedrals, when we are by profession pilgrims as well as project- and programme-planners, when our companions are children as well as chairmen and executives. The rewards will be ample for we inherit a world of dazzling meadows and shy deer and bird-calls. We own in a unique way the lake we ponder, the woods we explore and the gardens we admire. There is a quiet peace in our pulsing hearts, for we are free of phony appearances, the strain of posing, and the fear of being found out.

Even a cursory reading of the gospel illustrates that Jesus lived and acted out of this spirit. Docility to his Father, a self-emptying that enabled him to identify with the most human of his companions, and humility in every facet of his inner and outer life. The marks of his obedience. It began with Bethlehem and the conditions of his birth. It continued in exile and in the hidden life of Nazareth. His disciples were introduced to it, by the life-style they were called to assume. By the repetition of its message in parable and in symbol. He rode a colt in the only procession the gospel describes. He asked people to risk a personal encounter with him, rather than hide behind their suspicions and ideas of him. He embarrassed his disciples by his question: Will you leave me too? Can you drink the cup I drink? While he was vulnerable to the tactics of those who opposed him, he threatened them by his very veracity. Jesus left behind him a trail of shattered illusions and wrecked expectations. But he left no mistaken notions about his relationship with his Father and his commitment to those who were open and honest and unpretending.

Francis Bernadone understood the obedience of Jesus. As a youth he was forced by the pride and pressure of his father to make public his true allegiance. From that moment he was child of God, child of the universe, embarking on an obedience to the gospel. Our own conversion to such obedience need not be so dramatic. But it may involve similar risks. The scorn of those who consider insane any concrete effort to enflesh the gospel. The disappointment of those who had great hopes for us and for the mark we would make on our world. And separation from those who must reject what they cannot affirm.

Perhaps Francis missed one level of his vision in the church of San Damiano. But he didn't miss the invitation to docility. One thing Francis had not attempted up to that point in his life was building, in wood or stone. And suddenly he was gathering stones and repairing churches. It was only the beginning, of course, of his mission. From the stones of San Damiano to the highways and byways of Europe, to the assembling of friars, to a joint mission with Clare, to Rome for the launching of a movement of voluntary poverty and of obedience to the gospel. The seed of docility, the growth of a Franciscan spirit, inspiring and challenging our own jaded and hesitant hearts.

In the hours before his death Francis ordered his brothers to place his naked body on the naked earth. Sign of his relationship to sister earth and his acceptance of sister death. But sign also of the nakedness of his spirit, emptied of all vain-glory, identified with the soil from which he came, and intent, even in this final moment, on serving his Lord with great humility.

Obedience as fidelity

When I was nineteen and a candidate for the novitiate, we were given a booklet for study and reflection. Bold letters on the cover spelled R-E-P-J-U-B. It was my initiation into the mysteries and the demands of "holy obedience". In time I rattled off the anagram easily. I discovered that the obedience I was preparing to vow was to be: respectful, exact, prompt, joyful, universal, and blind. A heady lesson for a nineteen year-old. And heavier still in its implications. *Exact* meant precisely that. One was to terminate one's activity immediately at the sound of a bell, discontinuing even the downward stroke of a letter. And *prompt* was nothing less. Bounding from one's sleep at the call of the rising bell with the alacrity of someone escaping a burning bed. And *blind* was what it suggested. Planting cabbages upside down, if so ordered. Or, for me, tone-deaf and frightened of my own singing voice, leading the chanting of office in chapel, if so ordered. My memories of *respectful, joyful,* and *universal* obedience are less vivid!

Thirty years later I have quite different notions of my vow of obedience. Nor, to my knowledge, do the REPJUB books any longer exist. Over the years I have grown to espouse an obedience that is characterized by search and by listening and by fidelity. The search and listening are both personal and communal efforts. They embrace the entire gamut of God's mediators: scripture, creation, our times, other persons, and one's own heart. Fidelity is a lonely, often difficult, journey into the very core of one's vocation. To the place where God has instilled a sense of our own role in the building of the kingdom and the repairing of the church. A vocation entrusted to us, within the framework of whatever other choices we make.

Some of our choices are revocable, but the responsibility for our vocation remains intact. Our very integrity as persons demands that we place that unique life task before any other purposes or plans. Once we have accepted the call, we are committed to preserving and unfolding it, regardless of what changes around us or what adaptation we make in certain areas of our life. It is an awesome trust and at the heart of whatever obedience we promise or vow. Remaining true to that inner self and the fulfilment of its deepest longings constitutes fidelity.

There have been times in my life when I have questioned the truth of my community commitment and the truth of my participation in the Roman Catholic Church, precisely because of their conflicts with my own spirit of fidelity. No doubt there are Franciscans who left the Franciscan order so as to be free to pursue the spirit of Francis. And surely there are Christians who stand aloof from their institutional churches in order to create distance, and to regain a perspective on their own vocations. Sometimes disobedience, to the institutions of the church, the state, and the societies in which we live, is the only way to actual obedience to the requirements of one's own vocation. All institutions, of course, have grave problems with such dissidents and find ways to test and sanction such distinctions and decisions.

Vocations are individual and personal. Recall Moses and Abraham and Jeremiah and Isaiah. Recall John the Baptist and Mary of Nazareth and Elizabeth and Simon of Cyrene. Imagine the searching and the hard-won fidelity of Teilhard de Chardin and Mother Teresa and Dietrich Bonhoeffer and John Robinson and Hans Kung and Catherine de Hueck Doherty. Our inviolate covenants with God are forged in intimacy and ratified only by a life-time of tested fidelity.

I wish to say a personal word about the elements of obedience that I have depicted in this chapter. Humility, docility, and letting go have taken on a new meaning for me in the most recent stage of my life-journey. I accepted the summons to a three-month sojourn in India with mixed emotions. I think we are all attracted by what seems beyond us and bigger than anything we have yet attempted. I had never been outside the US until that December. Suddenly I found myself in Bombay surrounded by sounds and smells and scenes that I could never have imagined. I was in India for at least two weeks before I came to terms with my own fear and sense of displacement. I who wanted to believe that nothing human need be foreign to us was overwhelmed by the humanness and the foreignness of every detail of my life. It was difficult for me to recognize myself in that completely different world and to rely on the inner resources that had impelled me there to begin with.

It was scripture that first pierced my stiffness and feelings of unreality. For life around me opened up the verses of the psalms and the pages of the gospel as never before. The grain of wheat, the mustard seed, were close at hand. How many Samaritan women did I see at the well? How often I cast my eyes to the mountains, from whence came my help. Sheep and goats and fig trees were familiar sights. And the good shepherd had many faces. Water for feet-washing, day-labourers in the vineyards, the contrasting worlds of Dives and Lazarus were not images but reality. Gradually, I adjusted to food and climate, came to appreciate the eastern rituals and celebrations, learned to trust my surroundings, allowed myself to experience the stench, which continued to symbolize for me the poverty of India. And my spirit unbent and relaxed enough to allow the life and land of India to impregnate me and sow deep and lasting seeds. It was, in retrospect, a three-month lesson in docility, in doing what I could not do, adapting when I could adapt no more, and arriving at a new place inside myself where India and I could exchange gifts and charisms. India helped me to see my own country and my own style and habits of living in a new light. Confronted me with the arrogance of my own claims to simplicity and compassion. And continues to haunt me in the ways of obedience.

Two years ago I faced the crisis of cancer. The dreaded disease, which had already taken the life of two close relatives and invaded two others, now attacked me. In stark moments of confrontation with the truth, we can never predict our own response. At first I fell into a black hole, defeated. Then I swam in a sea of surrounding realities: my connectedness to others, my faith in the immensity of life, a strength whose source I simply accepted. In time my feelings roamed the spectrum of fear and despair. My body endangered by a mortal enemy. My life thrown into turmoil and my future made uncertain. My total helplessness in the face of a silent, aggressive foe.

My recovery was quick, my prognosis good, my basic attitudes healthy. I was immersed in understanding and love. My pain was borne by others and in that sharing there was comfort and hope. Before long I was engaged in all my normal activities. But "normal" has become a meaningless word. Health has become a relative experience. Time is etched with urgency. Life, which I too am prone to take for granted, has assumed a precious value. People and the time spent with them are treasures, not to be calculated, and not to be abused. It is a new era in my attentiveness to diet, to stress, to choices, in my relationships with others, and in the pursuit of my own vocation. Ultimately, the experience of cancer is for me an invitation to let go. To relinquish my claims on anything or anyone. To hold more carefully in open hands the gifts given me. But also to be more serious about following my dreams and to be less threatened by obstacles. Each day contains a certain amount of fear, and I am far from being reconciled to the possibility of future cancers. Sonehow, by the grace of God, in those early days of pain and realization I felt myself sustained by a faith in life's continuity. And I penetrated a bit further into the meaning of eternal love. Perhaps there is a kenosis-call in cancer that enables us to empty ourselves of some non-essentials, to identify more nearly with the human condition, and to embrace truth with less reluctance.

All the moments of Jesus' obedience led to his final journey to Jerusalem. The mission for which he was sent predetermined the hostility and resentment that gathered around him. His insistence on truth infuriated the established hierarchy. No one dared call them false guides or claim to have seen Abraham. No one dared embarrass them by giving sight to an obviously blind man or by restoring life to a local citizen, Lazarus by name. And then of course the supreme insult and blasphemy was his preposterous avowal of the intimate relationship between himself and God. How little did they understand the dynamic of it all! It was that very relationship and the energy it engendered that was the force behind all he said and did!

Images gather, creating the final scene. Opening up to us the meaning of obedience and its ultimate test. A towel girding the waist, image of humility. The reversal of roles, the Lord becoming the servant. The sharing of bread and wine, total identification with the simple. Images for a pilgrim people in their struggle towards freedom. And then the long day of Jesus' docility, in the garden, before Annas and Pilate, on the path to Golgotha, and upon the cross. Images of a long day into night, for the non-violent, the innocent victims of political schemes, the bringers of justice and the messengers of peace. Images too, of an empty tomb, of scarred hands, of a meal in Emmaus. And words: go to my brothers, to Galilee, go into the whole world.

The obedience of Jesus, which led him into and through death, reveals the pattern to be followed in the working out of our own vocations.

A eucharistic way of life

"But if I washed your feet, then you must wash each other's feet... as I have done, so you must do... Once you know all these things, blest will you be if you put them into practice" (John 13:14-15,17). All of us Christians, at some moment in the throes of our fervour, committed our lives to the needs and the defence of others. Whatever vows we have taken, they implied as much. Whatever promises we have made and ideals we set ourselves to follow, they implied as much. For what else do our words of profession and our acts of commitment mean? Jesus pronounced his own final vow at his last supper with his friends. In offering them his body and his blood in the bread and wine, he pledged himself to actualize that gift and that sacrifice. On that first Good Friday the Psalmist's words took flesh: "My vows to the Lord I will pay in the presence of all his people" (Ps. 116:14). I myself am the living bread, he had told his listeners. Whoever eats this bread will live for ever. It was difficult to imagine both what he meant by the bread of his body and by the eternal life it offered. The eucharist and the death and resurrection of Jesus are forever linked. His total act of obedience.

And still we find it difficult to believe the message of the eucharist! Especially to be obedient to the style of life our participation in it requires. For the ritual of the eucharist is preface to the action of the eucharist: the extending and the sharing of our bodies and hearts with one another, for the life of the world. "It is a searching, committing act to be involved in," John Poulton writes. "Bread set before us brings the starving into our company. Wine set before us brings the joyless, the sick and those who are denied the fruit of the earth."[4] The love promised on Holy Thursday is taken at its word each Good Friday. This prolonged event of Holy Week and Easter contains the gospel for our social order and for our personal lives. "Today we are celebrating our commitment to Jesus Christ;

---

[4] *The Feast of Life*, Geneva, WCC, 1982, p.20.

today we are renewing our commitment to the kingdom. And no one shall go hungry away."[5]

Our celebration integrates, therefore, the existential truths of our lives. We are people strung between birth and death, infinitely precious and politically dispensable, godlike in destiny and yet broken and even self-destructive. Our living gives visibility to both the magnificence of the divine creation and the bitterness of death, especially brutal, pointless, death. In us the holy one of God continues to grieve and agonize and dance and shout for joy. By our very immersion in our contradictory human journey, we bring the promise of life's continued triumph. By singing songs of liberation and of pilgrimage, we call attention to the empty tomb. By binding up the wounds of society's victims, we offer one another the testimony of scarred hands. By breaking bread and telling the stories of the mysteries that surround us, our eyes are opened to the companions travelling with us.

When the eucharist transforms our daily living, then dictators and death squads and advocates of nuclear weapons will not be able to destroy its ultimate power. The way of the eucharist is the way we follow in order to challenge everything that inhibits and reduces life. The way of the eucharist allies us with those who resist military regimes and police-states, who bear in their bodies the scars of intimidation and violence. In a eucharistic way of life we become one with the men and women and children who are living in the midst of death.

We are called to question the validity of our ritual and the integrity of our witness. To examine the complacency of our worship and our work, in light of the urgency and ultimacy of the life and death struggles around us. If the security of our private life-styles and of our structures is our prime concern, where is our willingness to be crucified with Christ? If renewal means new hymns and rearranged church furniture, then how serious are we about restoring unity to Christ's body? If society's outcasts cannot approach our churches, how clear is our connection with the one who was offered vinegar and who hung by iron studs? If our relationships and communities are

[5] Elsa Tamez, adapted for *Jesus Christ – the Life of the World*, worship book for the Sixth Assembly of the WCC, Vancouver, 1983, p.69.

exclusive and elitist, how can we claim association with Jesus, whose flesh was made available to the whole human race? If our churches are humdrum and tedious and encrusted with clericalism, how will the life-giving waters and the leaven ot sincerity and truth spill over into desert and barren places?

This is a difficult and daring obedience proposed for us. I for one have not paid my vow in the presence of God's people. Our cultural conditioning places us on the path of self-reliance and individual goals rather than corporate commitments and human solidarity. We fear pain and humiliation, and we shirk any identification with those who are marginal. We value power and prestige, and we have some reservations about the meek and the humble. We see ourselves as basically good and generous, and it is offensive to suggest that our actions betray our Christian profession. We acknowledge the necessity of conversion, while we admire from a distance those who choose the way of simplicity and political resistance.

Ultimately, our acceptance of an obedience to the gospel and to a eucharistic style of living depends on a single factor. The living truth of our relatedness to the God of life. We submit ourselves when we trust and we love. Obedience is the offspring of a deep and intimate relationship between our own hearts and the God who embraces us and who shares with us a joyous delight in and passionate concern for all of creation. When God is the one in whom we live and move and have our being, then our spirits will reverberate and our lives echo that limitless love. "How can we not obey what we love?... Shall I try not to sleep or to drink or to laugh? To walk out of his will is to walk into nowhere."[6] Then the mystery of Jesus' total obedience will be revealed to us. "As the Father has loved me, so I have loved you" (John 15:9). In obedience the word became flesh and lived among us. We claim to have seen his glory, the glory of an only Son coming from the Father, filled with enduring love. We aim to witness, by the obedience of our lives, to that enduring love.

Images gather. Broken pieces of bread, a cup spilled. A naked body on a naked cross. We prepare ourselves for the day when we fulfill our vow.

---

[6]C.S. Lewis, *Perelandra*, New York, Macmillan, 1944, p.116.

6. Freedom

The wind blows where it will. You hear the sound it makes but you do not know where it comes from or where it goes. So it is with everyone begotten of the Spirit (John 3:8).

The amazing truth of the kingdom is its availability. The kingdom is not for buying. It is not exclusive. It can't be hoarded. It succumbs, not to power, not to birthright, not even to the magnitude and sparkle of one's achievements. It is available to those born of the Spirit, those imbued with a simple faith. It requires one possession, freedom. The freedom to recognize kingdom-events and to follow a kingdom-course.

Freedom is...

Freedom is complete obedience to the element for which we were designed. The author of those words is now in her mid-seventies. My friend and I climbed the South Downs with her this year in England. She didn't remember that she had said it, two or more decades ago, in Uganda, to young missionaries. But I have remembered it frequently since I first heard it.

Complete obedience to the pursuit of truth. Not the truth of facts or of science, but the truth that is wholeness and integrity. And complete obedience to the calls and demands of love. For there is in each of us a potential nurturer and healer and tender lover and faithful friend. Freedom is complete obedience to the *special* elements for which we were designed. For some, the element of listening. For others, of being a bridge-builder, or bone-grafter, or a community-catalyst. Of fashioning meaning out of words or musical sounds, or out of movement. Of gardening or teaching or translating or pastoring. Just as discovering our element is the focus of our search and the key to our vocations, so is obedience to our element the entrance into freedom.

The question becomes for us: how far do we want to go into freedom? How serious are we about its bold discoveries and its perilous pitfalls? How free do we want to become? Jesus asked this question many times in different words. "What are you looking for?" he asked his first novices (John 1:38). "Do you want to be healed?" (John 5:6) and "What do you want me to do for you?" (Mark 10:51) were his questions to those seeking help. His parables and stories also posed the question. Do you want to go as far as the Good Samaritan? Are you more serious than the brother of the prodigal son? Can you take lessons from the flowers of the field and the birds of the air? Do you want to go as far as praying for your enemies and being consecrated in the truth? And what about the cup of suffering and the undeserved insults and the weight of the cross? Is your desire for freedom that wide and that deep?

The source of all our freedom is the freedom of Jesus Christ. By our association with him we are invited into the kingdom of liberation and love. We pledge our faith, "green as a leaf". We receive the spirit that disentangles us from sin, from the narrow perspectives of the law, and from the fetters of fear. We join all of creation in struggling to reject what is evil, in submitting to the greater law of love, and in sharing in the glorious freedom of those who belong to God. We become the recipients and the ministers of a new covenant, a covenant based, not on any written code, but on a relationship with one whose freedom frees us. In the space and spirit of that covenant we can gradually be transformed into the very image of Jesus Christ. Our freedom becomes our obedience to the very elements of Jesus' life, to the life of the gospel. We begin to make visible the fruits of the spirit of freedom: love, peace, joy, endurance, kindness, generosity, faith, mildness, chastity.

But the process of transformation, of growth in freedom, is inhibited by our inner struggles and our human weaknesses. Most of us wander far into the desert before we are certain that we won't go back to Egypt. We are slow in recognizing the false faces of freedom and of ridding ourselves of their allure. Only when we separate ourselves from the pseudo-freedoms of Egypt, that is, from the idols of our own day, can we make a clear choice.

Sometimes we deceive ourselves that freedom lies in the possession of things and of privileges. Freedom to travel to exotic places and to enjoy expensive gadgets. Desert-journeys point up the fallacies of such freedom. The creative use of the few resources the Indians had revealed to me a new face of freedom. Each part of the coconut was valuable: the milk we drank, the flower vase which the shell became, the pulp that found its way into our chutney, the mats fashioned from the leaves, and the fiber woven into the chain I wear. Nothing left over, nothing wasted, something to meet every need.

Power can also manifest itself as freedom. The budget I control, the committee I chair, the followers I have, the envy others feel for my position, my reputation, my charm. At the heart of Jesus' freedom was the refusal to build an earthly kingdom. He escaped those who would impulsively pronounce him king. When he had healed and fed, and nourished with his teaching, he quickly took a boat, and journeyed to the next village, or ascended a mountain to reflect and pray.

Sometimes we put our claims on people, mistaking possessiveness and dependence for freedom and love. It is then the desert of tested love, of willingness to suffer, of selfless giving, that reveals to us the mystery and the freedom of exchange. Whenever we are clutched by defensiveness and competition and fear, we know that we have strayed into the realm of false freedom. For each of these experiences closes doors and creates barriers rather than expands and connects us. In the desert of our inner lives we must wait again for freedom to disarm us and make us vulnerable.

True freedom unites rather than separates, relates us rather than isolates us. False freedom places us against others, against our environment, in a position of mistrust and of contest. True freedom places us with others, within our environment, in a position of mutual acceptance and of exchange. Test it for yourself. Are you free from worry when you carry a weapon into the forest or lock your money in a safe? Can you find the security you seek in a concerned community and in a respect for the world of nature? Is your freedom of movement dependent on a passport and credit card, or is it related as well to imagination and spiritual presence and vicarious experience? Is the person free who needs a first-class ticket or the finest aperitif? Is there not in all of us an envy for the one who travels with a knapsack and shares a picnic lunch with a companion? Is freedom from all responsibility for others true freedom? Or is your and my freedom enhanced by the burdens and joys we bear and share with those around us?

There is much to be said about the freedom we enjoy in our modern world. The marvel of twentieth century communications that connect us with remote places and spectacular events.

Much of the world can participate as spectators in the Olympic Games, the coronation of a queen, a papal visit, a World Council of Churches assembly. We are also, of course, brought close to the scene of a hijacking, the mutilated bodies in Sabra and Chatila, a tragic fire in Japan, and a truckers' strike in France. Hopefully, our awarenesses are heightened and our social consciousness stirred.

Many of us have opportunities for travel. Whether the purpose be business, personal, recreational, there is the possibility for exchange and mutual understanding. Books and art and cultural experiences of many types are available to us. We should be the most aesthetically and literarily formed of history's children. We profit by the conveniences and comforts engineered and marketed in our western world – from household appliances to medical advances. Meant to save time and energy and lives. The range of choices in every area of life is staggering and threatens to paralyze our ingenuity and creativity.

Within these freedoms, with their vast potential for human development and global unity, there lurks a heavy price. Not only do we become immune and insensitive to the barrage of news and information. Not only do we abuse our ability to travel, neglect ecology, and misuse our engineering skills. Not only do we cheat and compete and manipulate. But we in the west especially find ourselves struggling for space in a crowded, noisy world of technology and entertainment. We find ourselves malnourished and polluted by regular diets of cheap programming and tasteless advertising. We find ourselves trapped in a milieu that induces cancer, increases heart disease and produces frightening figures of death from suicide. What is the value of a society that drives its citizens to despair and early death? And what is the underlying illness of a society whose life-style and stress contribute to numerous and terminal malignancies? Are high blood pressure and the danger of a sudden stroke the price of our seasoned foods and our demands for fast and efficient output? Are our psychiatric wards and waiting rooms the price of conflicting values, and impersonal, desensitized living? Are our cancers and leukemias the price of a society gone berserk with its own power and bankrupt of spiritual and human controls? That which destroys our blood and triggers the growth of tumors lives first in the flesh and marrow of our society. In its abuse of the earth's elements, in its distortion and destruction of natural energies and foodstuffs, in its cruel and gruelling expectations of the human psyche. The symptoms and scars of the false freedoms of our western society are amply displayed in breastless women, chemotherapy victims, and hospices for the terminally ill.

Only when we have recognized our idolatries and returned to a sane and healthful style of living will our societies be reordered and reflect more spiritual values. Only when we have distinguished the slaveries of Egypt from the freedoms of the kingdom will we experience the latter's fruits.

Freedom casts out fear

True freedom, as true love, rids us of fear. In the economics of the kingdom, faith is sufficient. Faith the size of a mustard seed. The faith that is "confident assurance concerning things we hope for and conviction about things we do not see" (Heb. 11:1). The faith that recognizes the nobility of the poor and the beauty of the arthritic. In the spirit of such faith, one comes to a certain self-possession. And it is security and currency enough for life's transactions. If we possess ourselves, in truth and in humility, we need not fear what might be taken from us. For all else is bonus and non-essential. Anyone who has been given the kingdom need not fear the loss of lesser goods and more tangible riches.

Those who are afraid of being invaded or of losing something that belongs to them will emphasize their autonomy and their isolation. Those who are free in their possession of themselves can focus on loving and expanding, rather than guarding the entrances. They are less demanding of others' care and affection because they experience the freedom of reciprocity. Having found the way to freedom within, they find that no one has a harsh grip on their souls. They are unabashed by human pressure because they are free to follow their own conscience and insights. They can offer others their fullest and best selves rather than their obsessions, ego-centred ambitions, and self-delusions.

Authentic freedom leads us into the open light of truth, which in turn intensifies our freedom. We have all been in the position of the Samaritan woman whom Jesus met at the well. Guarding our own secrets, we've ventured curiously into the lives and affairs of others. How expert we are at times at cloaking our own shortcomings with our clever reasoning and our shallow criticism! Only when our cover is lifted and our hearts pierced do we stand face to face with truth and with the option of revealing our inner selves. The Samaritan woman was up to the challenge. She allowed the truth to enlighten her dark past and to heal her bruised spirit. So effective was the freeing truth that she became a spokesperson for the very process that had delivered her: "Come and see someone who has told me everything I ever did!" (John 4:29).

Freedom brings self-knowledge and allows us to stand firm in our own gifts and graces. To experience the harmony within that assures greater communion without. Freedom calls us to be at one with ourselves. To live in our bodies, not just occupy them. To acknowledge our greying hair and our failing memories. To inhabit our handshakes and our loving glances. To accept our limits and admit our mistakes. To recognize the need for confrontation, as well as the time for reconciliation. To remain broken in spirit, as well as to allow healing. To live with doubt and to fail at times and to refrain from endless self-criticism. Freedom provides the perspective to see ourselves in relation to others, giving and receiving, complementing rather than competing, forming partnerships rather than dividing spoils. Freedom gives us the courage to be human, to laugh at ourselves, and to risk the loss of our hard-won images.

Jesus faced Pilate and said: "The reason I came into the world is to testify to the truth" (John 18:37). His freedom was threatening to Pilate and to others who live in the distorted shadows of deceit and delusion. His open association with the prostitutes and suspicious characters of his time. His frank revelation of the sins of the Pharisees and the hypocrisies of the priests. His candid stories about unfaithful stewards and unforgiving debtors. His carefully honest answers to the insincere questions of those who would embarrass him. His strong words about his own origins and the source of his earthly mission. Jesus continued to speak the truth before the arresting soldiers and in the court of the high priest. In the end his testimony was heard and believed by a centurion and a fellow-criminal. The latter, with faith's desperation, asked about the kingdom. The first, with fear giving way to faith, made his own testimony: "Clearly this was the son of God" (Matt. 27:54).

Freedom is interdependent

If we dare to venture beyond the threshold of freedom, we will find ourselves in the company of a vast crowd. For our freedom is implicated in the lives and destinies of all those around us. "Remember that you have been called to live in freedom... Out of love, place yourselves at one another's service" (Gal. 5:13). One of the paradoxes of freedom is the way in which it engages us in the freedom of others. As long as some of our sisters and brothers are oppressed, our freedom is postponed. No one achieves freedom by a singular effort. The wholeness and maturity we struggle for in our private lives is dependent upon others' influence. Without support and prodding and guidance, no one of us achieves the goal of personal freedom.

Our freedom as a people is linked to the lives of men and women in all parts of our globe. And freedom is false if it denies the rights and limits the hopes of others. We are all called to participate in the struggle for liberation, in South Africa, in El Salvador and Guatemala, among the Native Americans and the homeless refugees. The struggle of the women of our world and the unemployed and the poor is our struggle. Gandhi was the living sign of this solidarity in the Indian march towards freedom. Martin Luther King voiced our interdependence as races and as members of one family. Many others in our own time summon the international community to place our common freedom on the line so that the most oppressed and most discriminated against may have hope.

Freedom is not a private search nor is it a lonely path. For Jesus it meant laying down his life as a ransom. For many Christians today it means imprisonment for the truth. For all of us it means the willingness to risk a bit of security and comfort so that others might know our solidarity with them. The road to freedom is crowded, with persons whose lives are violated by the tyranny and the torture of dictators. With persons scarred by dehumanizing experiences: in mental hospitals and welfare offices, with immigration officials and unscrupulous employers, and at the hands of insensitive pastors and priests. With persons whose hearts burn to provide a more stable future for their children. With persons who are asked to offer their physical lives for their faith and for the freedom of their brothers and sisters.

There is danger and there is risk in the path of those who seek freedom. But there is also hope and there are songs of celebration. The mighty thunder of footsteps that cannot be muffled. The plaintive chants of pilgrims who won't be ignored. Freedom is complete obedience to the element for which we were designed. Our dignity and our solidarity in all things human require that we take our place in that procession.

We won't be disappointed in the company we will discover. We will be surrounded by those who have understood the promise of the kingdom. They are the little ones, the "anawim". We go to them to learn the dynamic of freedom and to imbibe its spirit. Spend some time with children. Count among your friends and regular associates those who are poor. Learn from the sick and those who treat life as the gift it is. And observe true lovers, or better, become one. Such as these are sacraments of freedom in a world frightened by its own uncontrolled destructiveness and oppressed by its own denial of innocence and gentleness.

It was not by accident that Jesus placed a child in the midst of his adult followers and said: "Unless you become like this..." Spontaneous in your response to life, honest in your assessment of people, vulnerable to the world about you. Children are obedient to their element: innocent joy, eager trust, endless inquisitiveness.

The world has become a dangerous place for children. Sexual abuse, violence, neglect, are rampant. Children's art depicts their concern that adults will destroy their world before they have a chance to be negotiators and peace-makers. In some of our families today, children are bearing the burden of emotional support for their separated or career-bound parents. Confusion surrounds them: adults without faith, peers recommending drugs, material things increasing rather than allaying their loneliness and insecurity. If we will let them, children will lead us to the freedom that is their heritage. To creative day-dreaming, to wonder over truth, and into the Narnia[1] we seek.

---

[1] A reference to C.S. Lewis's *Narnia Chronicles*.

They will teach us something about limits and littleness, tenderness and transparency. And something about the upside-down kingdom where paupers become princes and cripples dance and Zaccheus has the best view. If we will be like them, we may yet grope our way back into an enduring hope and a sense of adventure, elements for which we were designed.

The lives of the poor, with all their stark deprivation, are uncluttered by superfluous words and goods. They have little, so what they have they appreciate. They live close to nature and they honour its secrets and observe its rhythms. They are pilgrims on a journey and companions in a struggle. "Happy are those whose strength you are! Their hearts are set upon the pilgrimage..." (Ps. 84:6).

I remember the spirit of the farewell celebration for the Cullen family before their deportation. An experience of the depth and breadth of the human community, multi-racial and multi-denominational, standing with two whose lives were committed to freedom. Often I recall the hours of an all-night vigil in Vancouver. Representatives from every region of the world assembled throughout the night to sing their songs of freedom and to testify, in prayer and pleas, to their belief in the eventual victory of life over death.

If we join them, those who know poverty will lead us further into their element. Further into the power of powerlessness and the strength of weakness. Further into faith and the meaning of prophecy. They will teach us something about the rough face of determination and the worn hands of sacrifice. And something about the upside-down kingdom where bread and fish multiply and the poor receive the good news and the Samaritan leper returns to give thanks. If we link lives with them, we may yet grope our way into a simple faith and a spirit of solidarity, elements for which we were designed.

The sick and the handicapped live face to face with their mortality. "Teach us to number our days aright, that we may gain wisdom" (Ps. 90:12). They have time to unravel the patterns of suffering and to weave the threads into a new cloth. They measure time with different instruments and plan their priorities with greater care. They know the sting of uselessness and the rewards of a transcending spirit.

Some months ago a friend and I visited a church headquarters in Illinois. Some of the people who were scheduled to meet with us had unexpected conflicts and were called away. One generous woman spent the entire morning sharing ideas and reflections with us, in spite of the ordeal she faced that afternoon. She had learned that her cancer was reappearing and would assess the situation with her doctor that day. Active and engrossed in her work, aware of the strain it placed on her family. Conscious of the failure of her previous treatments. She lived that morning as if life were full and her future unmarred. She gave us the benefit of her gentle and undefeated spirit.

Association with those who bear the burden of physical and mental handicaps tames us a little. They put us in touch with our own cowardice in the presence of pain, with the pettiness of our own problems, and our casual and careless treatment of our bodies and minds. They teach us something about the inner beauty of a resilient spirit. About patience and perseverance, and the infinite meaning of a single moment of life. About the upside-down kingdom where bones are mended and the blind see and where there is no taboo to touching the hem of gentle power. If we share their spirit, we may yet find our way to empathy and compassion, elements for which we were designed.

Those in love have a secret. Their gestures and voices and eyes communicate it. They rush to "wake the dawn" and warn the world of love's peculiar logic. They speak a new language and walk with new grace. They learn the dance of life, listening and opening, the rhythms of intimacy and ecstasy. They reverberate with the cosmos as it breathes in unison and blends the sources of silence and sound.

Those who love cross histories and heritages, continents and careers. They are deepened and hollowed out by mutual burdens and by a common cup of suffering. They wait with hope for love's direction. Freed by love's own dynamic, to be sifted and to die, to be made whole and human. Love is creative and those who partake are enlarged and made fruitful. They give birth to new networks and new visions.

Those who love teach us something about acceptance and abandonment, about pruning and profound commitment. And something about the upside-down kingdom where the stone rejected becomes the corner stone, where resurrection restores all lost life, and where human joy finds completion. If we are willing, we may yet discover the breadth and length and height and depth of the mystery of love, the element for which we were designed.

Crossing over

Often in life that which is a long way off is also close at hand. The universal and the cosmic are caught and reflected in what is unique and personal. A smile can be interpreted in any language. Grief is also translatable. Each of us is but a fragment of the universe, but each of us exemplifies the human story. The borders of our lives can be opened and our experiences enlarged, so that we become more than we are, so that we become human as well as female, global as well as nationally situated, ecumenical as well as grounded in a particular confession. It is possible to engage in a new dynamic with one's faith and one's culture by contact with, and entrance into, the larger life of our human community. The value of such a venture cannot be calculated. It represents a breakthrough into freedom and the beginning of a redemptive journey.

We live limited lives until we "cross over" into the concrete world of another country, another culture, another tradition of worship. I was stretched and challenged in so many ways by travelling and encountering people in India. Stunned by their ability to survive, overwhelmed by their hospitality, bewildered by cultural peculiarities: their politeness, their tolerance of slowness and inefficiency. I have been duly humbled by my language experiences in Switzerland, Germany, France and Italy. When I was an adult, I was forced to speak like a child. Never again can I take language for granted or impose mine on the rest of the world. And I have been enriched by the opportunities of sharing prayer and faith with persons of many denominations. Welcomed into a prayer meeting by Quakers. Served the eucharist by Anglican Africans and Lutheran women. Experiencing community in prayer with evangelicals and Protestant nuns and Orthodox priests. History comes alive and what is foreign becomes familiar. Vague images take flesh and understanding and appreciation grow. I have left forever a small world to live with the tensions and the tender mercies of God's larger family.

Contact with a world different from our own results in some relativizing and demythologizing. For a long time I have known that many people view our western ways and North American values with scepticism and dismay. I understand that better when I come closer to the people and places affected by our policies and practices. When I stand on British soil and look up into the awful bellies of US fighter planes. When a fellow Franciscan pledges to stand with her people in Nicaragua in the event of US aggression. When my Indian friends apologize for the poor quality of their tea, confessing that the finest products are exported to the west. I view with new eyes our western methods of communicating. The gross quantities of paper we consume. The constant rounds of meetings, some expensive, many sterile and full of game-playing. Our emphasis on sophisticated technology rather than personal sensitivity. It is enlightening to work with a cross-cultural group where nuances and body language are differently interpreted. Where English is not the dominant language. And where it is more important to understand one another than to complete an agenda or finish on schedule.

Entrance into another stream of history compels us to ask questions that can't surface in the insularity of our own familiar way of life. I saw the old and new sections of Frankfurt, West Germany, and realized that architecture tells the story of war. Similarly, the cement barriers protecting Switzerland's borders are obvious symbols of a world out of harmony with neighbours. Are we more complacent in the US about missiles and submarines because we have never felt the rain of bombs or the rumbling of tanks across our hillsides?

I stood in Winchester Cathedral in England and tried to voice my confusion. I saw an unbroken list of bishops from the tenth century to the present. What about the break at the time of the Reformation? What is the relationship between the current Anglican atmosphere and the earlier Roman Catholic leadership? My ecumenism falters as I find myself thinking in terms of "a break in continuity" and a "loss" rather than in terms of the progression of history and the constancy of people.

How do I reconcile the abundance of water in our western countries (toilet-flushing, lawn-watering) with the thirst I felt in India and my constantly dusty feet, not to mention the dehydration of thousands of babies? How do I reconcile the speed and peril of our highways, and our blatant consumption of gasoline, with the medieval transportation system of Madhya Pradesh, and the lack of machinery for farming?

Perhaps most significant and transforming of all is the crossing over into the lives of individuals, finding friends across all the limits of space and time. Faces from the Cameroons and Cuba, from Madras and Manila, a family in Oxford and another in Vancouver. Our lives brushed and we caught a bit of each other's spirit. In pondering issues of peace and justice, in celebrating our common faith, in hospitality and humour, we slipped through our divisions and planted seeds of unity and trust. I rejoice with the small group of Franciscans with whom we chanted vespers in Vezalay, France. And I grieve with my Sri Lankan brother whose family and country have been scarred by strife. My world is refashioned into a human circle. My life is freed of its narrow borders. And my spirit is engrafted with the spirits of those who journey with me.

Possibly no one was more versed in freedom's language or freedom's secrets than Francis of Assisi. He demonstrated it clearly in his unique relationship with the world of creation. Freedom meant harmony with his environment, and harmony meant kinship with the lowliest of creatures and the least in the human family. We sense how this realization flooded him as he roamed the meadows and roads of Italy, slept under the stars, and conversed with beast and bird, robber and leper. Harmony with his world made Francis a jester and a mystic, a dramatist and a prince. That rare combination of characters explains his unusual and radical freedom. He viewed the world upside down and that can indeed be freeing. He saw beyond the signs and sins of his times and read the designs of God, concretizing his vision into a rule of life. He injected a new spirit into the lives of his small company of followers, that of gratitude and reverence and humour. He welcomed every human being as a nobleman receives guests. He left them with a new feeling of importance and dignity.

Francis was free to recognize new patterns in the human web and free to rush foolishly into a life faithful to the gospel. He found freedom in his total commitment to poverty and in his unquestioned acceptance of suffering. To be free meant to copy, in one's flesh, the life and values and spirit of Jesus. He relived the gospel in the Umbrian Hills and in the stages of his own life's journey. Grecchio and Rivo Torto, the Carceri and Monte Alvernia: each recaptured a scene and a story from the life and lips of his master. He gathered into himself the free spirit of the poor and the wounded, of children and true lovers. He recognized the marks of the kingdom and he followed a kingdom-course. He crossed over the limits of his own time and place and presented himself to us as a challenge and a friendly guide, as our brother.

7. Exchange

The reign of God is like a mustard seed which someone took and planted in the garden. It grew and became a large shrub and the birds of the air nested in its branches (Luke 13:18-19).

The parable of the mustard seed has always been a particularly fascinating lesson. Something very small which grows and becomes so much more than anyone expected. Like the way our faith produces unusual results. Or the way our small contribution to a good cause multiplies and accomplishes more than we could have hoped. Or the way the "least" of our brothers and sisters become the holy ones among us. A parable about the value of the littleness of creation and the way that nothing is ignored or scorned in the kingdom of God. It is also a parable of exchange.

Making exchange visible

A world of exchange surrounds us. Even though most of the time we fail to perceive it. Or we feel as if we've made a most unusual discovery when our world "connects" and we see a particular pattern emerging. The secret of spirituality is the uncovering of this life of exchange, this very real and very visible interconnectedness that makes all of creation *one*. And then finding our own place in the "flow" of life, entering the mystery and becoming part of the universal "dance". Exchange, the dynamic reciprocity that flows between creatures, is the fundamental reality and we all have roles in its patterning and its stream. It is the link between uniqueness and diversity, maximizing both, and setting into motion the plan intended for the world and all that dwells within it.[1]

Think of a beautiful tapestry and the intricate and marvellous ways the many threads have become a whole. Each thread contributes to the colour and the design. The broken or missing thread upsets the pattern and the beauty of the weaving. Or think of a river, into which flow the many streams and rivulets from every direction. Into the depths and out into the dry land. A steady flow forwards and outwards, a commingling of waters.

---

[1] Rosemary Haughton has developed a theology of exchange in *The Passionate God*, a framework I found very helpful in pondering contemporary events and personal experiences (London, Darton, Longmann & Todd, 1981).

Each is distinct and each is contained in the whole. Images of the world of exchange that we live in and that reflect the completeness of exchange that is the Trinity.

Seasons follow one another, with a rhythm and reason deeper than our perceptions. The cycle of the trees, the cycle of a seed, of the living, throbbing world given to us as a parable. The snow in the mountains melts and waters the gardens far below. The skies provide rain and sun for the growth of the vines and the coming-to-birth of each red and white and yellow tulip. The leaves turn colour and fall and die, becoming mulch for the new planting. The blackbird mates and nests, the eggs are hatched and tiny creatures open their mouths for food. New blackbirds chant their vespers outside our windows.

Take up Psalm 104 and reread creation's song. Find the signs of exchange. Be aware of the patterns. Recognize the flow of life. Ponder the cycles. And give praise and thanks for the mystery that pervades the world of creation. "How manifold are your works, O Lord! In wisdom you have wrought them all – the earth is full of your creatures... When you send forth your spirit (the spirit that goes between all living things, the spirit of exchange), they are created, and you renew the face of the earth" (Ps. 104:24,30).

The challenge of renewal is to make visible the exchange that sustains and transforms all of life. It is the task begun at creation, interrupted in every age of sin (which denies the relationship and the connectedness of beings), the plan prophesied and prefigured. It is the task fulfilled again in the Incarnation. "The word became flesh and made his dwelling among us and we have seen his glory... of his fullness we have all had a share" (John 1:14,16).

Jesus became one of us, entered into our experience, took on our humanity, and opened the way for us to the Source. There can be no more concrete demonstration of Jesus' identification with us than taking on our flesh, speaking a human language, walking our roads, and experiencing our emotions. So that we might learn to live in exchange. "Love one another as I have loved you" (John 15:12). "Whatever you do for the least of my brothers and sisters, you do for me" (Matt. 25:40). "Wash each other's feet. What I did was to give you an example: as I have done, so you must do" (John 13:14-15). And during his last earthly meal, Jesus promised us that he would continue living in exchange. "Take this and eat... Drink from it, all of you" (Matt. 26:26-27). Let it be reminder and mandate to you, to offer yourselves for one another. Let it be my gift which remains.

Each of us who follows Christ follows a way of identification and of exchange. Each of us who drinks of the cup and eats the bread pledges to make real the gift which Jesus inaugurated, an ongoing life of service and surrender to the needs of others. We have committed ourselves to a way of living that connects us with our human family and incorporates us into the pattern of creation. A way of living that is marked by mutuality and reciprocity. By participation in the stream of life that flows among and between the people of the world, the creatures of the forest and the pasture, and the smallest living beings that cross our paths.

We are entrusted with the safeguarding of that flow and with making it transparent. It is a vast and awesome charge. If the human body, with its circulatory system and its intricate network of nerves, is a single entity connected and interdependent, then how much more mysterious is the interweaving of the universe, the movement of the stars and the tides, the complex variety of beings, and the interplay of the levels and life-cycles of all earth's creatures. Not a sparrow falls without it being known. Not a bomb is blasted without it having its effects on creation's balance. "For just as from the heavens the rain and snow come down and do not return there till they have watered the earth, making it fertile and fruitful, giving seed to the one who sows and bread to the one who eats, so shall my word be that goes forth from my mouth; it shall not return to me void, but shall do my will, achieving the end for which I sent it" (Isa. 55:10-11). How remarkable it is! How exalted and honoured are we, to be channels of exchange within this framework!

Some years ago when I was more directly involved with the formation of young women as new members of my community, I had a central theme for many of my classes and reflections. It was the fruit culled from my years of philosophizing. Everything is, in actuality, connected, and we spend our lives slowly discovering the inter-relationships. We are constantly amazed and amused to uncover another link that unites us to another being or that clarifies two sides of an issue. One of the great truths of philosophy is the "touch of the one in the play of the many".[2] For me now that view of reality, with its chief corollaries, the relativity of truth and being as process, was a two-dimensional view. The notion of exchange adds the vital element of movement, of flow, of energy passing back and forth.

Once we accept and explore the dynamic nature of human relating, we will inevitably dismiss some old patterns of perceiving and dismantle some of the structures that held up our world-view. Once we see the connections that enliven and enrich our interpersonal lives, we cannot return to a static and isolated notion of person. Persons are incomplete, made whole in exchange. Persons are communitarian, rather than individualists. Persons transcend themselves, find fulfilment in the reciprocity of giving and receiving. Hierarchies and distinctions (superior/inferior, higher class/lower class) become obsolete and unusable. The more appropriate image becomes that of a round table, with no corners and no reserved seats. Emphasis falls on interdependence and on the natural gifts that flow and transform the related parties.

Seeing and believing

Entrance into this perception of human reality and the realm of exchange requires faith. It is with the eyes of faith that we look beyond the external and the obvious, beyond the separations and divisions, and detect the common threads binding and uniting us. Faith looks, not to colour or creed, or role or title, not to age or sex or birthplace. But it sees the human features, the family likeness, the common yearnings, and the one body which includes all. Faith sees the unique and profound ways in which we are fitted and formed together, in which we complement and sustain and renew one another.

Thus Ruth was prompted to say to Naomi: "Wherever you go, I will go... Your people shall be my people and your God my God" (Ruth 1:16). And Jonathan felt his life depended on David. "He loved him as he loved himself" (1 Sam. 18:1). Thus Isaiah prophesied: "This is the fasting that I wish... sharing your bread with the hungry, sheltering the oppressed and the home-

---

[2] Rabindranath Tagore, *Gitanjali*, New York, St Martin's Press, 1962, p.59.

less... then he will renew your strength and you shall be like a spring whose water never fails" (Isa. 58:6-7,11). The gospel details the many dimensions and the fruits of a life of exchange. Also the costs. Once we have heard its message, we can never again object: When did we see you hungry or thirsty or naked or ill and not attend to your needs? Dives will always remind us of our ability to block exchange, as will those who refused the banquet, and the tenant farmers in the vineyard. We will be asked to repeat over and over in our own lives the multiplication of the loaves. To bear lasting fruit as branches of a single vine. To share in the hatred and rejection that all disciples of Jesus are guaranteed. To become the grain of wheat that, in dying, extends its life. We will be comforted by the knowledge that if we keep God's word, God will make a home with us.

We are all aware of the life we have received from others. How many bits and pieces of our present style of living and working, playing and praying, have we inherited from our parents and grandparents? We use the same recipes, celebrate the traditional feasts, enjoy the same music, share the same conscientious attitude towards our responsibilities. We have received life as well from our democratic predecessors, from the saintly people who taught us our faith, from those who settled and developed the region we live in. I remember a Trappist monk in Gethsemane, Kentucky, testifying that faith comes only through the living deeds and love of other persons. In his world, seemingly devoid of opportunity for human exchange, he acknowledged that very mystery.

I had a favourite teacher who awakened in me an interest in the vast world of spirit and faith. In the present, I live in the midst of a large clan, where nieces and nephews exchange generational views, and I feel the sustaining love of a close and caring family. The foundresses of my community have bequeathed us their charism and long is the list of those who have instructed and inspired me. My friends encourage my dreams and support my efforts. They give me the benefit of their trust and their affection. People who have died and those who now search with me the meaning of life touch me, with their example and their gift of self, and leave prints on my spirit. They move with me into territory I wouldn't enter alone. In the words of R.S. Thomas, "we peer at eternity through the cracks in each other's hearts".[3]

Each of us brings into this stream of human exchange what we have: ordinary offerings, unusual gifts, the united energies of our bodies and spirits. We bring our scars, our questions, our wisdom, our sexuality, and our faith. We enter all of it into the pool of life and we receive what we need. As we give ourselves away, we are completed. We fulfill what is lacking and find restoration and renewal. Charles Williams called it coinherence. "If this principle of exchange, substitution, and coinherence is at all true," he said, "then it is true of the whole nature of man... It is ordinary life which might be, more than it is, shot with this principle."[4]

It is exactly in the realm of ordinary life that we experience our relatedness and our interdependence. Our scars become the badge of our exchange and assure others that we embrace the human condition. My sister and I entered new levels of kinship and of understanding after we both faced and fought cancer. Comforting and credible are the worn hands and wounded hearts of those who lead us where we would rather not follow.

Our questions open up the darkened rooms we occupy and the hidden passage-ways of our escape. So that light and air may flow. Questions which challenge, which prod stubborn minds, which free us for dialogue and discernment. *Why* do you do what you do? What sustains you in your ministry? When and how will you make your word flesh?

We need the wisdom of those who have built our institutions and of those who believe they are now irrelevant. We need the exchange of insight between the easterner immersed in the intangible realities of spirit and the westerner whose life is pragmatic and productive. We look to the married to pass on the lessons of their exchange. We need the wisdom of the parent who remembers failure and rejection as well as the eagerness of the adolescent who rushes in where angels fear to tread.

Human exchange is bodily exchange. We use our senses to know and be known. A handclasp speaks clearly and forcefully. Love is conveyed through fingertips and embraces. The energy

[3] *Later Poems*, London, Macmillan, 1983, p.196.
[4] *The Image of the City*, London, Oxford University Press, 1958, pp.150-51.

that love prompts flows in our veins and seeks to share itself in an intimate and physical encounter. Love is creative and produces new life. Sexual exchange, with its rhythm of giving and receiving, deepens and confirms the spiritual commitment.

In our faith we bear one another's burdens, share each other's sufferings and consolations. We hold another person present, at a time of crisis or decision. It is a way of offering intercession. Contemplatives are involved in the mystery of exchange with a world exhausted of resources and in need of nurturing. We gather in faith to bless one another's missions, to give thanks for each other's gifts, and to pray for our enemies. In faith we celebrate the great rite of exchange, the eucharist.

Piercing the darkness

Three special influences contribute to our understanding of life's encounters and help make the element of exchange more transparent. They are the artistic, the contemplative, and the feminine. The artist leads us closer to the symbols and forms that undergird reality. The musician and the poet and the potter become one with the object of their art or the form they employ. In the encounter of artist and object a vision is inspired. There is an exchange between the landscape and the painter, the wood and the sculptor, the surrounding space and the soul of the dancer. The depth and force of that encounter determine the clarity and accuracy of the artistic expression. We who admire the art are also drawn into the encounter. And if we will, into an exchange with its inner meaning. Piercing through the veils of reality and communing with the inner world of the object of art, is the pain and the anxiety and the bliss of the creative person. Art enables us to live on different levels and to discern multiple meaning.

The contemplative also seeks communion with the object contemplated. Through a process of self-opening and self-emptying, the one who ponders gazes inside the mystery or the object at hand. He or she sees into and through the particulars of life to the underlying pattern and meaning. Contemplation is a mode of seeing and of listening. It is an intimate and concentrated act, aided by silence and solitude. It is an act of shepherding, "caring-for-being", as Heidegger defined it. It is intense and interrogative, seeking the deepest drops of beauty and meaning. With such vision, we attend to the awesomeness and the breath-taking quality of a summer sunset. In such a spirit, we approach the mystery of life and death, made visible in the peaks and the chasms of our human experience. We enter into a dialogue with the object of our contemplation, and as we perceive and pursue it, we are transformed. Thomas Merton describes a rare trip into Louisville: "Everything stirred me with a deep and mute sense of compassion... I went through the city, realizing for the first time in my life how good are all the people in the world, and how much value they have in the sight of God."[5] The exchange of contemplation precedes the exchange of compassion.

The feminine spirit, which is not synonymous with the female person, is sensitive to life's encounters and alert to the inroads they make in one's being. The feminine nature dwells easily in the darkness of earth's soil and of life's deep seas. It has a certain familiarity with roots and springs and the basic elements of air and fire. Open to the mystery and the meaning that lurks in life's cycles and in human responses. A certain resonance with the wisdom of the unconscious and the language of silence. And a certain attentiveness to the flow of time and the harvesting of life's fruits. A spirit energized and made creative by relationships and community ties. The feminine spirit waits in readiness for the opportunity to inject breath into the clay of existence and to humanize the daily affairs of life. Open to all expressions of exchange and channel of its vital flow. It is the feminine contribution to the rich array of spiritual and human gifts. Such a spirit can be awakened and reinforced in each of us.

Microcosm and macrocosm

The mystery of exchange is just as real in the broader life of our communities and churches and societies. As on the level of persons, it can be neglected and obstructed. Often at meetings I become conscious of the possibilities for exchange and lament the gaps that remain unbridged. We occupy rooms with the same people for hours at a time and leave with no sense of their feelings. We discuss issues and ideas and become embarrassed

---

[5] *Sign of Jonas*, New York, Image Books, 1956, pp.97-8.

by personal applications or personal stories. The medium of meetings has blended into our anonymous, theoretical mode of existence and we are losing its potential for exchange. We don't have time to pause and question the speaker or gather our own honest reactions. To peer at faces rather than phrases. To study the human dynamic rather than last month's minutes. To launch each person present with new energy rather than appoint another committee.

The very value of a community lies in its possibilities for exchange. As a whole we are greater and more effective than the sum of our individual parts. We have the opportunity to complement one another, to form balanced teams, to experience the rhythms of action and reflection, solitude and participation. Those with talent for teaching, prophecy, administration, mutually support one another. Those who earn salaries can supply for those who minister among the poor. Those who are healthy can take the places of those whose strength has been drained. And those who are retired become the sources of power and prayer for the missionaries and leaders. In an international community like my own, there can be an exchange of cultures and of resources and a mutual redemption. Every community needs its corn-harvesters and wall-menders. And its Fredericks, those who gather sun and colour and build stories.[6] It is precisely this variety and diversity that make a community a living, connected unity, rather than a mere congregation. The poets and the hermits and the dreamers are as vital as the workers and the wage-earners. For all renew and enrich one another.

Parish life thrives when there is a spirit of exchange between clergy and laity, men and women, the experienced and the initiates. When there is exchange as well with the institutions that surround it, and links with the political and social life of its members. The Christian life entails experiences of solidarity with other members of the body of Christ. It leads ultimately to a "transference of pain"[7] from one part of the world church to another so that together we make up what is lacking in Christ's body.

---

[6] The reference is to *Frederick* by Leo Leonni, New York, Random House, Inc., Pantheon Books, 1967.

[7] J.L. Wilkie, "Comments on Melbourne Conference on World Mission and Evangelism", Melbourne, May 1980.

The privilege of the ecumenical movement is its opportunity for exchange. I personally have had experiences within that context that I have not had in my own church. The recognized leadership and ministry of women. The unique resources of Orthodox spirituality (the wisdom of the desert fathers, iconology, monastic asceticism). Probing the scriptures with Anglicans from South Africa, Mennonite pacifists, and Moravians from Surinam. Outside appreciation for the vitality and creativity of renewal in the Roman Catholic Church and for the ecumenical spirit of my own community. How much further we could go into the deep life of the Spirit, which unites and renews, if we trusted more and would risk more! What gifts we could still exchange, in formation efforts, in missionary endeavours, in greater hospitality on the local level, and in an open eucharist! If we had enough faith in our true identity as members of one body!

It is individual human beings who comprise our legislative bodies and armies and embassies. Nations and governments will never foster exchange and interdependence until their members do. Threats and accusations, deterrence and espionage, turn a world of exchange into a world at the brink of annihilation. My own country boasts of its superiority in the manufacture and transfer of arms. More military equipment passes through our borders than educational supplies or medical provisions. The exchange most nations know best is currency exchange.

Such an atmosphere at the national and world level promotes in turn the defensive and reactionary attitudes of many citizens. The notion of "privatism" is in direct opposition to a life of exchange. We become defenders of private property, private interests, private income. And even private rooms and private appliances. Fear is the fruit of privatism. And fear blocks freedom and exchange.

There are occasional breakthroughs in this system of exclusion and competition. We do have exchange programmes for students and scholars and cultural groups. Some towns and cities have companion-counterparts in other parts of the world. There are ambassadors of good will: peace groups, women's groups, missionaries. There are also a growing number of persons who seek and discover the connections that open them up to new levels of exchange. Persons who are learning a theology of letting go, for the sake of those who have less. Persons who distinguish between the human families in Russia and the US and their governments and defence ministries. Persons who bring together the burning issues and problems of today and the direct, honest, criteria of the gospel. Persons who build bridges, by their words and deeds, so that we can cross over to one another and embark again on the adventure of exchange.

What could we envisage if human hearts burst wide and all the energies and gifts stored up in them were released, for use among the members of the human family? Gandhi projected just such a consideration: "The atom bomb is the acme of physical force and, as such, subject to the law of dissipation, decay and death that governs the physical universe. Our scriptures bear witness that when soul-force is fully awakened in us, it becomes irresistible. But the test and condition of full awakening is that it must permeate every pore of our being and emanate with every breath that we breathe."[8]

The resources of the north would close the gap of hunger in the south. And the south would show the north the value of a simpler, more friendly, society. East and west would exchange secrets of literature and philosophy and enter into dialogue about a safe world and the security of healthy and honest debate. Churches would experience a mutuality in ministry, recognize one another's priesthood, and be revivified by the energy that emanates from their common sources. Local churches would look to the world church for clues about their mission. And the world church would find its hopes restored and its life rejuvenated. The whole church could turn together to the gospel and reform itself into a church of the poor. Communities would challenge their corresponding societies to a more human future by their own experiments with new systems of governing and value-formation. Men and women would use their talents to build a strong community, and patterns of paternalism and resistance would yield to creative ministries and spiritual renewal.

The rich and the poor would find in each other a part of their own redemption. Less land would lie fallow. Big empty houses

---

[8] *All Men Are Brothers*, New York, Continuum, 1980, p.90.

would be filled. There would be shoes for all, more bodies
would be healthy, and self-pity and loneliness would be
diminished. Everyone need not be whole, for there would be
willing legs to compensate the lame and eager eyes to complement the blind. Young people would be the strength of the old,
and the elderly would be confidants and counsellors of the
young.

There would be a more even distribution of work. Small
home-industries would flourish and latent skills would appear.
Families and communities would build their own homes, bake
their own bread, and provide their own entertainment. People
who had enough money and means would actually work for
nothing, or vacate their positions in favour of others. There
would be a greater interest in a safe and harmonious environment and a respect for water and air and earth's resources.
Everyone would speak more than one language. The media
would report all the news, good as well as bad. Communication would improve, words would have their meaning restored,
and gifts would be authentic signs of exchange. The word
stranger would disappear, along with borders and passports
and visas. Suffering would be divided by its sharing, and many
would feel the honour and joy of a few. There would be
dancing in the streets and even in churches as a natural
expression of celebration and unity. All of us would sense the
oneness of the body and our common call to be its builders and
menders.

A spark that blazes

There is nothing to prevent us from investing our lives and
embarking upon this upside-down scheme of things. Nothing
but our fear and our lack of faith in the potential of Gandhi's
soul-force. "You are a chosen race, a royal priesthood, a holy
nation, a people God claims, to proclaim the glorious works of
the one who called you from darkness into marvellous light"
(1 Pet. 2:9). Priesthood is our vocation. In the Latin sense of
"bridge-building". And in the Buddhist sense of sainthood. A
Buddhist saint repairs roads and builds bridges so that people
can come together. We have the power to connect Spirit and
breath, roots and dreams, sparks and fidelity. The sign of our
covenant is a colourful bridge, a rainbow. Persons are

"ordained" priests in each moment of encounter. And grace flows with the daily drama of exchange.

Likewise hospitality is our vocation. The pages of the gospel abound in examples of this form of exchange: the story of Mary and Martha, the Good Samaritan, the parable of the wedding banquet. "The one who welcomes you welcomes me, and the one who welcomes me welcomes God who sent me" (Matt. 10:40). Originally hospices were houses of rest for travellers and pilgrims. The original sense is maintained today, especially in the east and in Europe, in hostels for youth, in "pensions" for those who journey, for those away from home and family. Frequently on my travels I have been touched and inspired by the graciousness of those who share their homes, offering water for bathing, a hot meal, and the bed of one of the members of the family. Not because I am an old friend, or a distant relative, or even a casual acquaintance. But because I am on a journey and have a need. And because I bring into their homes a bit of my own world and offer them a brief span of my time.

In the US especially we have converted what was intended to be a time and place of exchange into the paid service and anonymous atmosphere of hotel and motel. We are less apt to open our doors to strangers and to inconvenience ourselves and expose our privacy. We have lost a vital source of friendship and of trust and unity. Perhaps we can still regain a portion of this treasure. By being more spontaneous in our invitations to share a simple meal or spend a quiet weekend in our spare room. By becoming within our neighbourhoods a centre of prayer and of refuge for those in need.

Priesthood and hospitality, specific moments of human exchange, are rooted in relationship. Micah summarizes it well: "This is what the Lord requires of you: act justly, love tenderly, and walk humbly with your God" (6:8). They are interwoven and integrated in a life of exchange. A global village, a personal history, and a life of prayer.

Walking humbly with God is prayer in the broadest sense, for I hesitate to speak of prayer in any other way. Prayer is like breathing; it is that close to the rhythm of life. It is our openness to the sacred and the transcendent, to the pattern of exchange in the here and now. And our response to the movement of the Spirit in our midst.

Seeking silence, standing still in reverent attentiveness. Time, say the Navajo Indians, is not determined by a wristwatch or interrupted by a phone. The instrument that measures it most nearly is the sun. Time is a rhythm of life, not a ticking that quickens the nerves. "Morning after morning he opens my ears that I may hear" (Isa. 50:4). What chaos would we chance in our lives if we trusted the timing of the sun rather than our wristwatches?

Walking humbly with God enables meaning to emerge from the darkness. The agony of a suffering friend. The strong spirit clinging to a dying body. The power of healing hands and the gentle oil of anointing. Sensing in our disturbed peace the stirrings of the Spirit. Celebrating a cosmic liturgy. Holding the fullness of night's beauty. Glimpsing the Artist in a world white with snow. The holiness of gnarled hands and of joyful tears. Singing in our hearts and new vigour in our limbs.

Prayer flows in and out of our experiences, our beliefs, our witnessing, integrating and naming them. Enlarges our notion of sacrament. Cracks open the secrets of nature and reveals our reflection in the eyes of our travelling companions. Prayer tests our spirit, thrusts us into conversion. Calls us to stand back and own our creatureliness. Calls us to sweat and strain under our human yoke. We pray when we have the courage to do what we most want to do. When we have the humility to be grateful for the goodness that abides in creation. When we weep with the sorrowful. When we heal the wounds we have in common with the entire world. When we leave people, not to escape them, but to learn again how to find them. When we go deeply into our own wells so that others may drink from our fresh waters. When we voice to one another our heaviest burdens and our greatest longings. When we remember and gather those whose passion is being enacted, those who walk the final steps to Golgotha.

Most of us want above all to learn to pray. To be healthy and mature enough, honest and humble enough, to exchange life in that way. To be liberated by silence. And transfigured by contact with the glory of God. To communicate at that deepest level with all who belong to God and to us, in love. To be filled with the fire and the wind of the Spirit.

There is in the depths of each of us a yearning to live life fully. To plunge into the limitless waters of love and exchange.

To fulfill our vows and incarnate the words we speak and the professions we make. To enflesh the gospel in some small way with those with whom we journey.

During these final days of writing a friend and I have stood in Francis' footsteps in Assisi, invoking his assistance and imbibing his spirit. We were attracted to the little church of the Portiuncula, dwarfed by the basilica that contains it. It was at the mountain retreat of the Carceri that we felt closest to the heart of Francis. And it was in the humble church of San Damiano, where Francis' mission began, that we heard anew our own call to rebuild Christ's church. We sensed again that the way is one of littleness and prayer and humble service.

From Assisi we went to Taizé to celebrate the special feast of the "invisible third party" who has stood between us in these pages and who stands between each of us and a life of complete obedience. With thousands of pilgrims, the majority of them youth, we awaited the flame and the fresh wind of Pentecost. We sensed again that the Spirit embraces all, that no life is insignificant, and that peace is the distinctive gift.

How clear it is that the human family yearns for a glimpse of the holy and to be grasped by the Spirit of God! Ask those who kneel at the tomb of St Francis or who participate in the late night chants at Taizé what it is they seek. A spark in their own lives of the fire that blazed in Francis' spirit and prompted a worldwide movement of conversion and peace-making and commitment to the poor. The empowerment of the Spirit that transforms visions and dreams into bold proclamations and faithful witness.

The streets of Assisi still echo with the sounds of Francis' followers. The fields of Taizé are dotted with pilgrim tents. The word becomes flesh again in Port Elizabeth, South Africa, La Palma, El Salvador, and in Warsaw, Poland. And we, like Moses, are called to step aside, to stand in amazement before the burning bush, and to respond. God said: "Remove the sandals from your feet, for the place where you stand is holy ground... Come now! I will send you to Pharaoh to lead my people out of Egypt" (Exod. 3:5,10).

Other Recommended Spirituality Titles

Quiet Places with Jesus
40 "Guided Imagery" Meditations
for Personal Prayer
Rev. Isaias Powers, C.P.

This best-seller sets forth Isaias Powers' "guided imagery" meditations for personal prayer. "Guided imagery" cuts through busy schedules, harried nerves, and daily distractions. It taps the hidden power of our memories and imaginations to influence thought patterns. This prayer method releases the Spirit within us, lifts our minds to a "quiet place" and turns our hearts to God. *Quiet Places with Jesus* offers 40 such guided meditations.

Three helpful appendices assist the reader/prayer even more. The first provides additional material on prayer and meditation. The second correlates specific problems with appropriate meditations in the book. The third arranges the meditations in a manner particularly for use in Lent.

Letters From An Understanding Friend
Jesus on the Way to Jerusalem
Rev. Isaias Powers, C.P.

This is the most personal journal from Isaias Powers made public to date. Now his readers can glean insights into the special place that the multifaceted passion of Jesus holds in this spiritual writer's own prayer life.

Powers stretches Jesus' passion out over the last year of the public ministry, not restricting it to its culmination on Calvary. The "journey to Jerusalem" theme from Luke's gospel triggers this collection of "forty letters from the Lord."

By assigning a personalized correspondence as his literary device, the author delivers a poignant survey of Jesus' compassion for his contemporaries and for those suffering psycologically, physically, and spiritually in our times.

Available from your local religious bookseller or directly from:
Twenty-Third Publications, P.O. Box 180, Mystic, CT 06355

Other Recommended Spirituality Titles

Beyond Loneliness
A Practical Christian Response
Edward Wakin, Ph.D. and Rev. Sean Cooney, Ph.D.

The authors show how to face loneliness and to learn important things about ourselves, by understanding how loneliness affects us personally. They identify ways in which we can respond to loneliness positively and to make it a part of feeling, responding, and growing as Christians.

The approach is vivid and original. The result is a unique guide that will help everyone deal with loneliness and assist those who want to help the lonely.

Out of this realistic treatment of a difficult topic comes a positive message: we can reach beyond loneliness to a fuller life of faith and hope. This book shows how.

Creation and Human Dynamism
A Spirituality for Life
By Rev. Joseph Donders

This volume was written in Africa. The author contends it is in the African primal beliefs that life is received and celebrated as it was intended to be. The confrontation of those beliefs (so near to the primal vision of the Old Testament) with our contemporary world, makes the intentions of Jesus so much more understandable and enjoyable.

The first part of this book shows how the Old Testament invites us, in the name of God, to put human life in the center of our interests, even the center of our worship. The second portion is about Jesus opening totally new dimensions in our human life. He recreated the whole of humanity in one family. He recreated the entire economic, political, cultural, ecological, and social order of creation. The third section of Donder's presentation works these dimensions into a practical spiritual plan of action for believers today.

Other Recommended Spirituality Titles

Refreshment in the Desert
Spiritual Connections in Daily Life
Rev. Gilbert Padilla

This deeply spiritual book delves into the Gospel message of love, forgiveness, and prayer. The short, moving meditations are for adults thirsting for an awareness of the presence of God in their lives.

These forty-one excursions into the quiet desert of one's soul and heart help the active person put behind the rapid pulse and demands of work, family, and community for a short time each day.

With this contemplative silence the author's meditations invite individuals to listen more closely to what is going on inside themselves, and to discover God's grace-filled call to respond to his nurturing presence. The desire to respond is one's prayer. And it blossoms in refreshing insights into spiritual connections that sustain, fortify, and offer a positive faith-perspective upon daily life.

The Gentle Touch
Charles J. Keating, Ph.D.

This book surfaces universal human questions in a profoundly personal way: "Who am I? Is life worth living? Why? What makes life significant? Where is joy? What does death mean? How do I make sense out of failure? What do I mean whan I say I believe? Do I need to believe? Is there life beyond family? If so, what does it look like? Why is it important to relate to others? What does the future hold for me?"

This reflections-provoking book of spiritual essays invites adult readers to meet life's common experiences with an eye toward discovering within them a source of meaning and strength.

Available from your local religious bookseller or directly from:
Twenty-Third Publications, P.O. Box 180, Mystic, CT 06355

Other Recommended Spirituality Titles

Prayerful Pauses with Jesus and Mary
William Peffley

This book offers quiet reflective moments, unburdened by superfluous words. The verse sculpts images of Jesus and Mary in the mind and heart. The poetry opens doors to prayer previously locked tight within the soul.

Prayerful Pauses with Jesus and Mary becomes a poetic life of Christ, a meditative New Testament, a liturgical sweep from Advent to the ascension, a rosary companion. But at most it frees the heart and mind and soul to be closer in thought and prayer to Jesus and his mother.

Mary at My Side
Msgr. Robert Guste

This sensitive volume is a heartfelt and personal testimony of experiencing a spiritual relationship with Mary the Mother of Jesus.

It is an evolving story of the author's discovering in Mary his most significant help in fostering a relationship with her son, Jesus. Guste affirms an attention and devotion to Mary, which has as its sole rationale and purpose being led to Jesus and ultimately to God the Father.

In deeply moving frankness *Mary At My Side* portrays Mary as a prime example and model to all who feel called to respond to Jesus in their lives. The book focuses upon the mystery and attraction of Mary within historical and contemporary expressions of spirituality. Special attention is paid to the impact of the traditionally accepted apparitions of Mary at Lourdes, Fatima, and Guadalupe. Guste also shares insights into the rosary and other prayer forms and devotions associated with Mary.

Available from your local religious bookseller or directly from:
Twenty-Third Publications, P.O. Box 180, Mystic, CT 06355